MW01088359

# CHILTON'S GUIDE TO
# AUTO BODY REPAIR and PAINTING

Robert D. Harman

*Step-by-step repairs for rust, dents, scratches*

Vice President and General Manager JOHN P. KUSHNERICK
Managing Editor KERRY A. FREEMAN, S.A.E.
Senior Editor RICHARD J. RIVELE, S.A.E.

CHILTON BOOK COMPANY
Radnor, Pennsylvania
19089

Copyright © 1983 by Chilton Book Company
All Rights Reserved
Published in Radnor, Pennsylvania 19089 By Chilton Book Company


Manufactured in the United States of America
    4567890      210987654


Chilton's Guide to Auto Body Repair and Painting
Robert D. Harman
ISBN 0-8019-7378-3 pbk.
Library of Congress Catalog Card No. 79-8307


Originally published under the titles of Minor Auto Body Repair, Chilton's Minor Auto Body Repair, and Chilton's Minor Auto Body Repair, 2nd Edition by Robert D. Harman, 1975, 1979, 1980.

**SAFETY NOTICE**
Proper service and repair procedures are vital to the safe, reliable operation of all motor vehicles, as well as the personal safety of those performing repairs. This book outlines procedures for repairing vehicles using safe, effective methods.

It is important to note that repair procedures and techniques, tools and parts for repairing motor vehicles, as well as the skill and experience of the individual performing the work vary widely. It is not possible to anticipate all of the conceivable ways or conditions under which vehicles may be repaired, or to provide cautions as to all of the possible hazzards that may result. Standard and accepted safety precautions and equipment should be used when handling toxic or flammable fluids, and safety goggles or other protection should be used during grinding, cutting, sanding, prying, or any process that can cause material removal or projectiles.

Before substituting another tool or procedure, you must be completely satisfied that neither your personal safety, nor the performance of the vehicle will be endangered.

# Contents

Chapter 1    **GETTING STARTED**    1
Tools and Equipment   3
Auto Body Repair Kits   5
Basic Method   6
Key Steps to Auto Body Repair   21

Chapter 2    **REPAIR ONE**    22
Minor Surface Scratches   22

Chapter 3    **REPAIR TWO**    26
Deep Scratches and Minor Dents   26

Chapter 4    **REPAIR THREE**    33
Small Fender Dents   33

Chapter 5    **RUST PROBLEMS**    44
Preventing Rust   45
Do-It-Yourself Rustproofing Kits   46

       **REPAIR FOUR**    51
Repairing Rust Holes   51

Chapter 6    **REPAIR FIVE**    63
Creased Panel and Door Edge   63

Chapter 7    **REPAIR SIX**    71
Dented Trunk Lid   72

       **REPAIR SEVEN**    83
Dented Hood   83

Chapter 8    **REPAIR EIGHT**    88
Crumpled Rear Quarterpanel   88

Chapter 9    **REPAIR NINE**    103
Damaged Door and Front Quarterpanel   103

Chapter 10    **REPAIR TEN**                                  **113**
                        Fiberglass Panels   113

Chapter 11    **REPAIR ELEVEN**                              **124**
                        Vinyl Tops   124

Chapter 12    **REPAIR TWELVE**                            **129**
                        Aligning Body Panels: Doors, Hoods & Trunks   129

Chapter 13    **REPAIR THIRTEEN**                          **132**
                        Removing Headlights, Tail Lights & Lenses   132

Chapter 14    **REPAIR FOURTEEN**                        **142**
                        Installing Adhesive Body Side Molding   143

                        **REPAIR FIFTEEN**                        **148**
                        Installing Rivet-On Body Side Molding   147

Chapter 15    **PREPPING YOUR CAR FOR A NEW PAINT JOB**    **151**
                        Step 1: Cleaning   152
                        Step 2: Spot Priming and Featheredging   153
                        Step 3: Sanding the Complete Car   162
                        Step 4: Masking the Car   166
                        Step 5: Getting the Car Painted   170

Chapter 16    **PAINTING TECHNIQUES**                    **171**
                        Refinishing Systems   172
                        Surface Preparation   174
                        Aerosol Cans   177
                        Spray Guns   178
                        Blending New Paint   180
                        Special Problems   181
                          Clear Coat Paint   181
                          Stone Resistant Coatings   182

Chapter 17    **BODY CARE**                                **183**
                        Washing   183
                        Cleaners, Waxes and Polishes   184
                        Buffing   186
                        Caring for Chrome   189
                        Interior Care   189
                        How to Remove Stains from Fabrics   190

# Acknowledgments

The Chilton Book Company wishes to express its sincere appreciation to the Marson Corporation, Chelsea, Massachusetts 02150; The Oatey Company, Cleveland, Ohio 44135; PPG Industries, Ditzler Automotive Finishes, Southfield, Michigan 48037; Repair-It Industries, 436-440 Hopocan Avenue, Barberton, Ohio; Larry Speer; Ritt Jones Collision, Prospect Park, Pennsylvania; Silvatrim Corporation of America, South Plainfield, New Jersey 07080 who gave their assistance and expertise in the preparation of this book.

Original photography by Lillian Harman and Kerry A. Freeman

# 1

# Getting Started

Most minor auto body damage can be repaired by the owner of the vehicle Minor auto body damage falls into 5 general categories: (1) small scratches and dings in the paint that can be refinished without the use of body filler, (2) deep scratches and minor dents that require body filler but do not require pulling the dent out or hammering it out from behind, (3) dents and deep gouges that require pulling the panel back into shape and then filling with body filler, (4) rust holes and (5) lightly crumpled panels.

There are many reasons for wanting to repair your car's body yourself. Perhaps you enjoy working on or around your car or truck. Maybe you want the vehicle to look its best before you try and sell it. Some owners discover that their older model is in good mechanical condition and that doing some minor body work is far cheaper than going in hock for a new model. If you are carrying a higher collision deductible on your insurance policy, you may want to repair a minor dent yourself rather than deal with the insurance company. Or, you simply may not feel that the price the local body shop wants to fix that rust hole is worth it to you. Whatever the reason(s), you can repair minor damage yourself, using the actual repairs in this book as a guide. Everything you need, except the materials, is here. All the work photographed in this book was done with readily available tools and materials.

All of the step-by-step repairs involve basically the same steps, and you should be able to find one that approximates the repair you wish to make on your vehicle.

## DECIDING WHAT TO DO

The first step is to decide what you want to tackle yourself.

It makes no difference what panel you are repairing. Hoods, doors, fenders and rear quarter panels are all the same when it comes to body repair; they are stamped into their shape in a press. When you make a dent in one, you stretch the metal. If you stretch it too far, it either requires a new panel or special equipment to repair it. The biggest mistake most do-it-yourselfers make is stretching the panel more, in trying to repair it, than it had been with the dent in it. As a result, they end up

Use common sense. If the repair is too big, don't attempt it yourself

with a bulge instead of a dent. When you do this, you have twice the trouble you had when you had the dent, and if you don't have access to special equipment and some very special talent, you could get in big trouble.

You must use common sense. If the job is too big or if the panel is stretched badly, don't try to repair it. You could end up with a larger project than you had originally. And no body man likes to pick-up where somebody else left off, and try and undo their mistakes. It takes longer and is more costly in the end.

There are many ways of deciding what to do yourself or what would be better to have done professionally, but the answers to these questions will go a long way to making your decision for you.

1. What is the extent of the damage?
Carefully assess the damage relative to the repairs and procedures in this book. Use common sense—many repairs are not as hard as they look, but if the panel is severely misshappen, torn or mangled, don't attempt it unless you have plenty of time and the vehicle is not worth a great deal. When assessing the damage, be sure to check carefully for hidden damage that is not readily apparent.

2. How many and what kinds of tools are required to do the job?
At the beginning of each repair in this book, we've listed the tools that are necessary to make the individual repair.

3. Consider the value of your time.
How long will the car be out of service? How long will the work take? Each repair in this book is also accompanied by an estimate of the time required for a person of average mechanical ability to make the repair using commonly available tools and materials.

4. How much will it cost YOU to make the repair?
Get several estimates from body shops and compare these with the cost of do-it-yourself tools and materials. Each repair lists the materials you'll need to make the individual repair.

5. Do you plan to sell the car?
Will the repairs you make help sell the car? Will the repairs you make help get more money for the car? Remember, that if the work is done professionally, the higher cost of the repair must be deducted from your profits.

6. Do you plan to keep the car?
Will the repairs increase the value of the car? Will this repair mean that future repairs will be less likely (for instance checking the spread of rust)? Can you afford NOT to make the repair?

7. Consider the age of the car.
Is it worth spending more money to have the work done professionally, or is the market value of the car less than the cost of a professional repair job?

8. Consider your insurance policy.
Is the cost of a professional repair less than the collision deductible on your policy, so that you will wind up paying for the whole thing anyway? If so, consider saving what you can, by doing it yourself. Also consider the effect on your premiums by reporting a minor accident that may not have been your fault. You can save insurance premium money over the cost of the repair by repairing minor damage yourself.

If you've considered the answers to these questions, you've probably concluded that you can save a good deal of money on minor body repairs by doing it yourself. You may already be familiar with some of the skills necessary, but even if you're not, you can easily develop these with a little practice and patience.

# TOOLS AND MATERIALS

The first thing to do is to assemble the tools you will need. They are inexpensive and readily available at most auto paint supply stores, auto parts stores, discount stores, and mail order auto suppliers. You might think that for a small job on a door or fender, it would seem silly to buy any tools. Look at it this way. You probably have a claw hammer hanging in your garage or a quarter inch drill with an assortment of drill bits, etc., which you don't use every day of the week. So there is nothing wrong with having a few inexpensive body tools hanging that can pay for themselves time and again.

The basic tools for minor repair are as follows:

Body hammer

Dent puller (depending on the repair)

Sanding board

Sanding rubber block

¼ in. drill w/drill bits

Half round plastic file

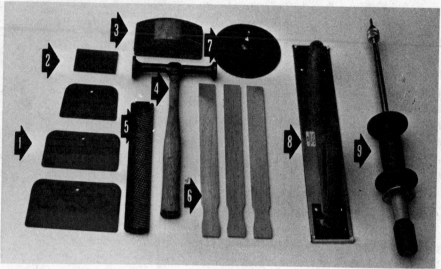

1. Three assorted spreaders
2. Glazing squeegee
3. Standing block
4. Body hammer
5. Plastic file
6. Paint paddles
7. Grinding attachment
8. Sanding board
9. Dent puller

Package of plastic spreaders
Putty squeegee
Grinder attachment for drill
Paint paddles

Materials you need for your first job:

1 quart auto body plastic, with tube of hardener
1 tube of glazing putty
1 can of aerosol lacquer base primer
2 5 in. grinding discs (24-grit), used on drill
6 17 in. × 2⅔ in. sanding paper (36-grit), for sanding board
6 17 in. × 2⅔ in. sanding paper (80-grit), for sanding board
3 3¾ in. × 9 in. sanding paper (36-grit), for hand use
3 3¾ in. × 9 in. sanding paper (80-grit), for hand use
3 3¾ in. × 9 in. sanding paper (100-grit), for blocking
1 gallon lacquer thinner, for tool clean up

―――――――――――――――― CAUTION ――――――――――――――
Most of the products you will be using contain harmful chemicals, so be extremely careful. Always read the complete label before opening the containers. When you put them away for future use, be sure they are out of children's reach!

You won't use up all these materials on your first job, but they can be used at a later time. Put the lids and caps on them when you're through, and store them away for future use. Perhaps if you do a good job on your car, you'll be using them on your neighbor's car next week. Ever think of that? (Don't do it too cheaply though.)

# AUTO BODY REPAIR KITS

If you are just beginning in auto body repair, you may be unsure of exactly what kinds and amounts of materials are required for a given job.

Most manufacturers of auto body repair products began, supplying materials to professionals. Their knowledge of the best, most-used products has been translated into body repair kits for the do-it-yourselfer. Kits are available from a number of manufacturers and contain the necessary materials in the required amounts for the repair identified on the package.

Kits are available for a wide variety of uses, including:

rusted out metal

all purpose kit for dents and holes

dents and deep scratches

fiberglass repair kit

epoxy kit for restyling.

Kits offer the advantage of buying what you need for the job. There is little waste and little chance of materials going bad from not being used. The same manufacturers also merchandise all of the individual products used in this book—spreaders,

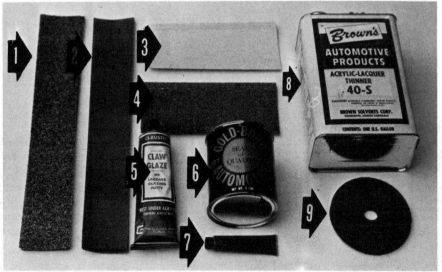

1. 17 in. x 2-⅔ in. sanding
   paper (36-grit)
2. 17 in. x 2-⅔ in. sanding
   paper (80-grit)
3. 3-¾ in. x 9 in. sanding
   paper (100-grit)
4. 3-¾ in. x 9 in. sanding
   paper (36- and 80-grit)
5. Glazing putty
6. Plastic filler
7. Hardener for plastic filler
8. Gallon of lacquer thinner
9. 5-in. grinding discs
   (24-grit)

Auto body repair kits contain all the materials in the proper amounts for specified repairs

dent pullers, fiberglass cloth, polyester resin, cream hardener, body filler, body files, sandpaper, sanding discs and holders, primer, spray paint, etc.

# BASIC METHOD

Now you're ready to begin. All repairs discussed in this book involve more or less the same basic steps.

## Study the Damage

Take a few minutes to study the damaged area. Try to visualize what shape or contour it had before it was damaged. If the damage is on the right fender, go around and look at the left fender. Study the lines of the panel, and then try to think the problem out. Even professional body men get into trouble on small jobs, because they start swinging a hammer before they study the damage. There is no substitute for using your head.

If there is access to the back side of the panel so you can use a hammer to bring the panel back, fine. If not, you will have to bring it out the best you can from the outside. Until now, I haven't mentioned the most important tool a body man has, and that is the palm of his hand. By laying your hand, palm down and flat, on the panel, you can determine a lot of things you can't even see.

Let's categorize the two types of repairs we will be making. The first are the door dings, stone dents, or in other words, dents that are so slight that there's no point in trying to metal finish them i.e., to bump them out. For dents that fall into this category, just grind the old finish back and fill them with plastic. Follow the steps

Learn to identify body panels by their proper names

at the end of the next category, beginning with, *Preparing the Panel for Plastic Filler*.

The second category is the one that requires the most care. This is where the novice can get into trouble. Let's assume you have a fair size dent in your front fender. As you look at the damage, try to visualize how the damage was done. You might say to yourself, "The point of impact was here and the angle of impact was about thirty degrees to the rear." Try to figure how the dent was actually made. In most cases, to repair it you follow the reverse in pulling or hammering it out. Let's assume again that you can get to the back side of the damage with a hammer or pry

Arrow shows good example of stress line. Pull or hammer out along this line

bar and you begin working the metal back to its original position. Go slowly. Work a little at a time. This is where the palm of your hand is so very useful. When the dent is close to being back to its original shape, lay your hand flat on the panel and slowly slide it back and forth. Get your body behind your hand, and as you move your hand across the panel, think where the highs and lows are. THINK STRAIGHT. Be sure your hand is flat, as you can tell nothing by feeling with your finger tips.

## Using the Dent Puller

Quite frequently you'll find that there is no way to get behind a damaged panel. Now the dent puller comes into use. Study the panel carefully and determine where the lowest spot is. This is usually the best part to pull out first. Quite often

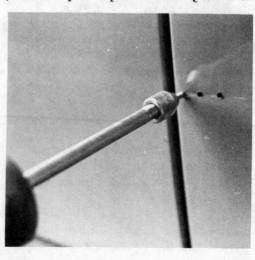

Using the dent puller. On a small dent like this, be careful not to pull the metal out too far. Just a few light taps with the puller in each hole will suffice

there are stress lines in a damaged panel. Once you learn to read these, you will be well along in learning sheet metal working. Stress lines usually run from the lowest part of the damage toward the outside.

Using a ¼ in. drill and a drill bit about half the size of the end on the dent puller, drill a series of holes along the stress lines to the lowest place in the dent. Make a few trial pulls and carefully watch what the panel does. Since no two dents are the same, you can't be told exactly where to make your pulls. If you watch what the panel is doing when you put tension on it, you can tell whether or not you are pulling in the right place. If it looks as if you should move over a few inches, drill more holes and try it. The important thing to remember is not to be in a hurry.

Later in the book, there is a series of step-by-step repairs to various panels. It may be helpful to compare one of these jobs with your own.

## Working the Panel Out: Go Slowly Here

The important thing to remember, when working the panel back to its original shape, is not to push or pull it out too far. That is the reason we put so much importance on going slowly on the first couple of jobs. On a small area it is fairly easy to determine whether your damaged area is very close to its original shape by using the palm of your hand as I described before. If the area is quite large, however, such as the whole length of the panel, a trick used by a lot of body men is to take an ordinary yardstick and lay it flat across the repair area. Yardsticks, the kind you get from the hardware stores and lumber companies, are very flexible and will curve over just about any panel—including contoured ones. Lay the yardstick flat over the area and slide it up and down the panel. Watch the edge of the yardstick that is against the metal. High and low spots may now be seen very easily.

When you are finished bringing the panel out to its original position, low spots shouldn't be more than one quarter inch at the deepest point. There are shops that

Using a yardstick to find highs and lows on a large area is an old body man's trick. Use it when straightening metal and when filling in with plastic

allow much more variation than that, and there are shops that insist that the panel be even closer than one quarter of an inch. If you don't get your panel close to original, the plastic filler will be much too thick. In a few months it will begin to crack and will have to be redone. I once had an old timer tell me when I first went to work for him, "I don't care if your plastic work is thick, just so it isn't deep." Keep the plastic as thin as you can. Plastic was designed to take the place of lead when it became too expensive and panels became too thin to be reshaped with heat. It was never intended to be used for filling large low spots.

Now, compare your work with some of the photos, and when you are satisfied that you are as close as you can get, then start with the second phase.

## Preparing the Panel for Plastic Filler

Insert the grinder attachment into your ¼ in. drill and put on one of the 5-in. grinder discs. You should wear safety goggles. If you don't have them, put on a pair of light shaded sun glasses. Most ¼ in. drills don't turn at a dangerously high RPM, but the chips and dust can very easily get into your eyes.

Grind the old finish off the damaged area. You will have a hard time getting all the paint off in areas where you have done some pulling, especially around holes you've drilled. Do the best you can. If you have a wire brush for your drill, this sometimes does a good job around such places and in other areas that are inaccessible. If you are working around a bumper or chrome molding, it is a good idea to put several layers of masking tape over them in case you should slip during the grinding operation. This will also keep the plastic, which can be very hard to get off, from getting on them. Leave the tape on until you have completed the job.

As you grind back the old finish, be sure to go three or four inches away from the damaged area, so that there won't be any plastic on top of the old finish at the edges

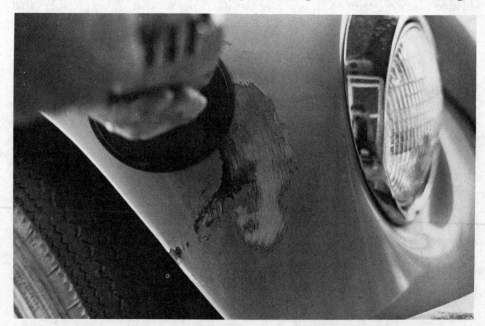

Using the ¼-in. drill with a grinding attachment. Always use safety precautions such as a three prong electrical plug and glasses

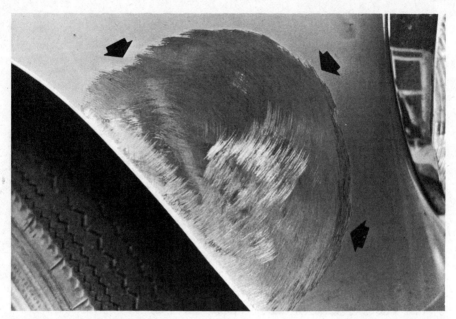

Arrows indicate how the old finish is ground back several inches from the damage. This gives you plenty of working room

of your repaired area when you're finished. When you take the car to the paint shop and the painter looks at your work, there won't be any question in his mind that you know what you're doing if there's no filler on top of the paint. Plastic on top of the paint edge indicates an unprofessional job. To explain this as simply as possible without getting into the technical end of the painting process, if your plastic filler work goes out beyond the old paint edge, the finished panel will have an ugly ring showing right where the plastic starts and ends. If the painter has to work right up to the edge of your filler, there is always the chance of his getting low spots in your repair with his air sander. All the effort you made to get a perfect job will have been for nothing and you can't blame the paint shop.

## Mixing and Applying the Plastic

Now we're ready to "mud" the panel. Make a mixing board out of a piece of cardboard box. Open your package of plastic spreaders and select the size that seems to fit the situation. For larger areas, you would use a larger spreader. After you have read the label on the can of filler, open the can. Using one of the paint paddles, remove enough material to apply a medium coat to the panel and put it on the mixing board. Apply the correct amount of hardener from the tube and thoroughly mix it. This is tricky. The correct amount of hardener is dependent on many factors—temperature, humidity, etc. Too much hardener will cause the filler to harden before it is applied. Too little hardener and the filler will not cure properly. When using hardener, it is better to use too little than too much. This gives you more working time and less chance of getting lumps in the mixture.

As you first apply the plastic, take small amounts on your spreader and sort of wipe it into the metal. This insures that you will obtain good adhesion and is called *tinning* the metal. After the area is tinned, go ahead and spread the plastic in

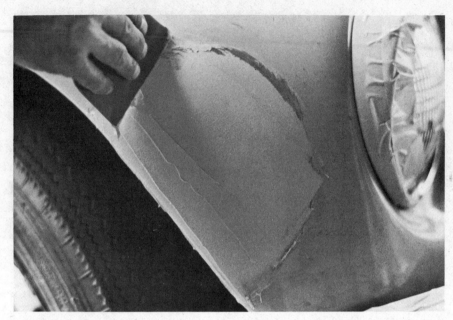

Spreading plastic is simple once you get the hang of it. Apply plastic smoothly and quickly, and then allow it to harden

smooth, even strokes. This is important. Spread the material on as smoothly and as quickly as you can. When you have a fairly smooth coat, leave it to dry. As soon as the plastic turns to a solid state (about the consistency of soft rubber) take your plastic file and, very lightly, knock off any high spots. Don't file too heavily, though, as the file will dig in and pull the plastic loose from the metal. After you've done this,

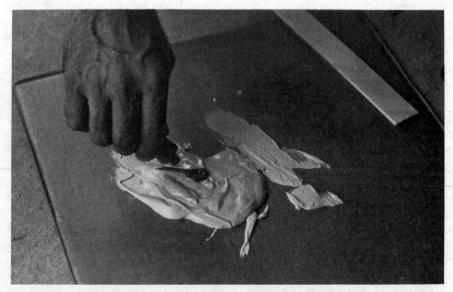

Mixing the hardener into the plastic takes practice because temperature and humidity determine how much hardener to use. Too little is better than too much

Mix the plastic thoroughly before applying it to avoid soft spots in your work

let it set up for about fifteen to thirty minutes, depending on the temperature and the amount of hardener you used. One word of caution here. Don't spread the plastic on and then go in to eat lunch, because when you come back, the filler will be hard as stone. If you don't work the plastic in stages as just explained, your labor will be doubled. It is ready for filing when you can barely nick the surface with your fingernail.

After the plastic has set for about half an hour, it is time to work it down with the

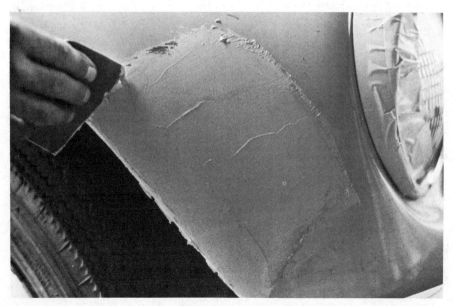

Learn to apply the plastic quickly. Once you get used to it, there is plenty of time to tin the metal with small amounts on your spreader

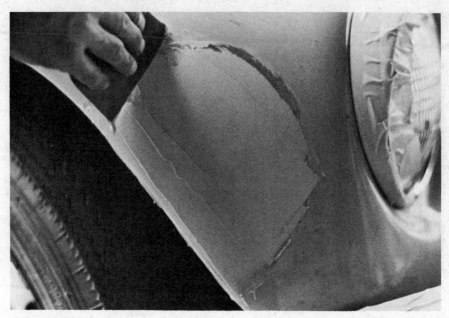

When making your final strokes, try to follow the contour of the panel. The smoother you apply the plastic, the easier the rest of your work will be

sandpaper. If the area is very small, use the rubber block and a piece of 3¾ in. x 9 in. (36-grit). If it is large, use the sanding board and a piece of 17 in. x 3¾ in. (36-grit). Sand the plastic smooth, watching that you don't get the area too low. This is just the first coat so if you notice low spots and pin holes in the work, don't worry

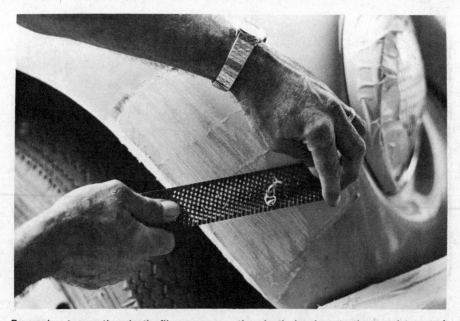

Remember to use the plastic file as soon as the plastic hardens to the consistency of rubber. If you wait too long to file, your work will be doubled

about it. When you first start sanding on fresh plastic, you will notice that the sandpaper tends to clog. Use a small knife or similar object to flick off the specks from time to time to keep the paper from completely filling up. After you have gotten the area to about the right height, wipe the panel with a clean rag and recoat it with another application of plastic. You will notice that this time the material will go on much smoother and you will have more control when spreading it. Just as before, get it smooth and then *leave it alone*. Repeat the procedure you used on the first coat with the file and then allow it to set up hard. Now, work the plastic down with a sanding block or sanding board to one sixteenth of an inch of the desired finished height.

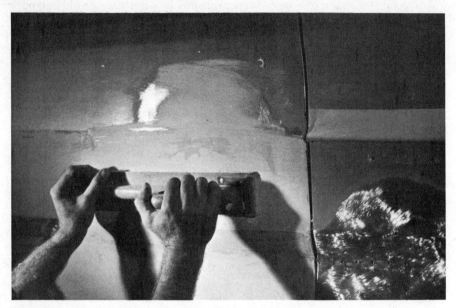

Using the sanding board to work the plastic down

Now, change your paper to the 80-grit and continue to work it down to the finished level. Knowing when to stop with the 36-grit and start with the 80-grit will come to you after a few times. The beauty of it all is that if you get too low with the 80-grit, you can always apply another coat. If you have trouble telling whether you are too low or too high by using the palm of your hand, grab the yardstick again and use it to spot the voids. It works just as well during this stage as it did when you were bumping out the panel. Usually a second or third coat on the damaged area is the standard for a good body man, but if it takes you five or six, don't worry about it. You're new at this.

THINK STRAIGHT. The important thing is to learn to read what the palm of your hand tells you as you run it over the panel. Running your hand back and forth rapidly over the panel, won't tell you a thing except that it isn't straight. Your hand will automatically tell your brain that it feels lumps and waves. Watch your hand as you move it slowly along the repair and concentrate on what is high and what is low. Let's say you're very close to having the panel perfect. It's a natural tendency to think that this is good enough, and when it is painted, it won't show. WRONG! Painting not only DOESN'T HIDE, IT HIGHLIGHTS DEFECTS.

This is where the amateur can often do a better job than a lot of body shops. Most body men work on a percentage of the total labor of every job; therefore, the quicker they finish one job, the quicker they can start another. If it is not perfect (just close); instead of "hitting it" one more time, they turn it over to the painter. Most body men know from experience how much they can get away with, and if the shop doesn't insist on perfect work, the customer gets a sloppy job. Since time should not be one of your motives, there is no excuse for anything but perfection.

## Priming and Glazing

When you are sure the panel is straight, when it looks good and your hand tells you it is good, let's take one more step to insure it is not only good, but perfect.

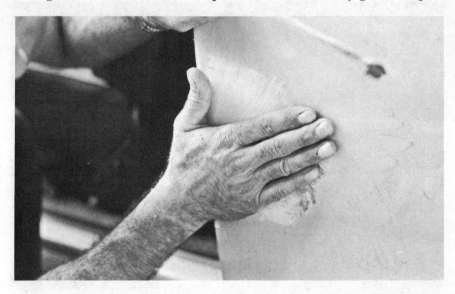

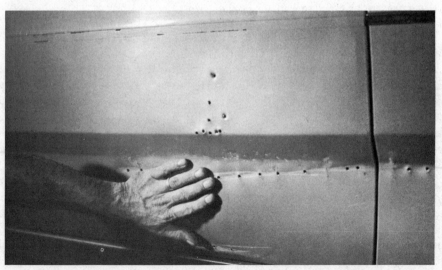

Learn to use the palm of your hand as a gauge. It's one of the body man's most important tools

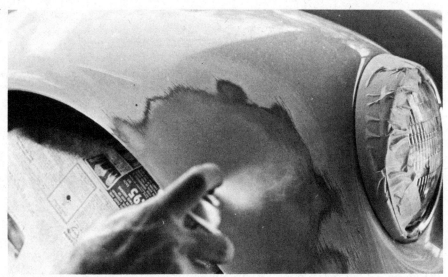

Allowing the first medium coat of primer to go way beyond the edge of the old finish just wastes material

Take a clean rag and wipe the panel clean. Now, shake the aerosol can of primer thoroughly as per the instructions on the label. Apply a medium coat of primer over the area you have just repaired. Be sure all the plastic is covered and just a few inches of the metal surrounding it. Don't go way out on the metal and onto the old finish edge, as you will just be wasting material. Let the primer dry; thirty minutes is usually sufficient.

When the primer is dry, take the small rubber squeegee and the tube of glazing

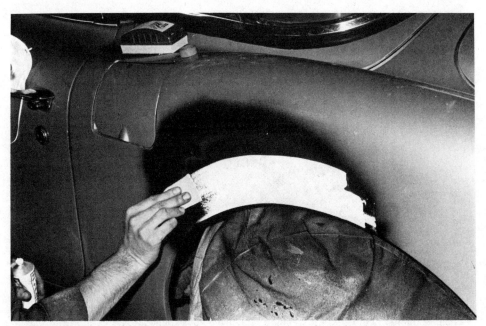

Apply body putty in long, even strokes

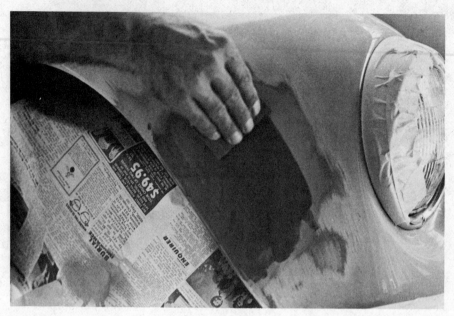

Apply glazing putty in one stroke applications. If you go over what you have already spread you will tear the previous application away from the surface

putty and apply a thin covering of putty over the repaired area. Apply this material smoothly and quickly. You will notice that if you go back over an area that you had puttied just seconds before, it will tear the film of the first application. This material must be put on in one stroke applications and then left to dry. In other words, squeeze about a tablespoon of putty onto the edge of the squeegee and immedi-

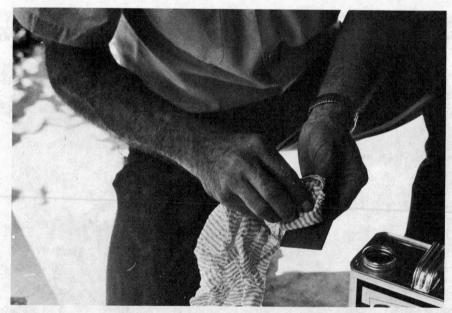

Lacquer thinner is the best for cleaning putty from your squeegee. Be careful with this liquid, though, as it is more flammable than gasoline

Folding 100-grit paper over shortened paint paddle for use in blocking glazing putty

ately, with one quick stroke, apply it the length of the repaired area. If there is still
some putty on the squeegee after the first pass, drop down and wipe it on right
below the first pass. When you have the area covered, leave it to dry for about an
hour.

Clean the squeegee at once with lacquer thinner and a rag. If it takes longer than
an hour for the putty to dry, you probably put it on too thickly. The purpose of
glazing putty is to fill sandpaper scratches, small low spots in your work, and pin
holes in the plastic.

When the putty is dry, take a paint paddle and cut it to nine inches with a wood

After the putty has dried, block sand with the shortened paint paddle and 100-grit paper.
This removes scratches and small low spots

saw or a hack saw. Now, take a piece of 3¾ in. x 9 in. (100-grit) sandpaper, and fold it over the shortened paint paddle lengthwise. Lay the covered paint paddle flat on the puttied area and sand it down until it is smooth. When you finish sanding, there shouldn't be very much putty left on the panel, as it was only applied to fill sandpaper marks, pin holes and very minute low spots. You should see most of the primer that you previously applied. I like to think of putty as nothing but thick primer. In the old days of body repair, scratches and voids were filled by priming heavily and sanding, sometimes as many as five or six times. With glazing putty, you do the same thing in one operation. When you have finished sanding the area with the paint paddle and the 100-grit paper, take another piece of 100-grit paper and fold it in thirds lengthwise. With the folded paper in your palm, very lightly go over your work with long smooth strokes.

Finish sanding with a piece of 100-grit paper folded in thirds. Use long even strokes. Sand very lightly

Don't sand in any one spot but in long strokes the entire length of the repaired area. If you dwell on one spot, you will lose everything you have gained and finish with a wavy job. Take a clean rag and thoroughly wipe the area. Now, get down close to your work and carefully inspect it. Look for any imperfections or pin holes that may still remain. If you see any bad spots, get the putty and squeegee out and do these spots individually, with just enough material to do the job. In other words, if you see a few pin holes, wipe the putty into the holes flush with the surface rather than put a big gob on and have to go through the blocking procedure again. These areas should dry in just a few minutes. When dry, sand them down smooth with 100-grit, being careful not to overdo it and damage the adjacent areas. Wipe the area down again and prime the entire area with a medium coat. When you apply the primer this time, prime over the old finished edge a couple of inches. This will prevent the metal from rusting until it can be painted.

# KEY STEPS TO EASY BODY REPAIR

1. Study the damage before you start.

2. Try to imagine how the damage was done.

3. Work the panel back to shape slowly. Take your time.

4. When grinding back the old finish, go far enough so that no plastic will be on the old finish when you're through.

5. Learn to use the palm of your hand. A good body man can't work without it.

6. Don't depend on paint to hide anything. If you can feel it, you will definitely see it when the job is done.

7. Glaze small imperfections in your plastic work—pin holes, scratches and very minor low spots with smooth quick strokes.

8. Block your glazing with the paint paddle and 100-grit sandpaper.

9. Prime lightly, covering all bare spots to prevent rust.

# 2

## REPAIR ONE

# Repairing Minor Surface Scratches

Just about every car or truck has minor scratches, superficial rust spots or other surface imperfections in the paint. These 2 rust spots on a Blazer fender were caused by spilled battery acid, and can be easily repaired in this stage without the use of body filler, before they rust through the sheetmetal.

---

**REPAIR 1**

## Repairing Minor Surface Scratches

**TIME REQUIRED:** 30 minutes–1 hour

### TOOLS

No hand tools required

### MATERIALS

\*Clean rag or tack cloth
\*Solvent
\*320 and 400 grit sandpaper
\*Primer and paint
Rubbing compound
Masking tape and newspaper

\*Starred items are packaged individually or in kit form by major manufacturers of auto body repair products and are available from auto supply and accessory stores.

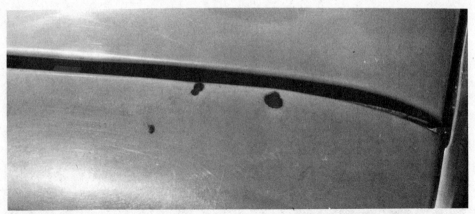

Step 1. Minor scratches and surface rust such as these can usually be repaired without using body filler

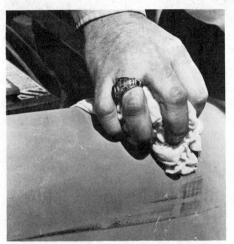

Step 2. Wash the area to remove all traces of dirt and road grime. Wash it with a Prep-Sol, Formula 409 or some other solvent to remove the coating of wax, so that the paint will stick

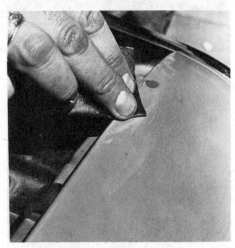

Step 3. Small rust spots and scratches like these require only light hand sanding. Start with 320 grit

Step 4. Finish the sanding with a piece of 400 grit wetted from a bucket of water. Wet sanding will feather the edges of the surrounding paint. For large areas you should use a sanding block, but it's not necessary for small jobs

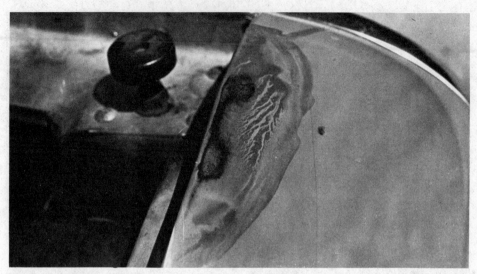

Step 5. It should look like this when you're finished wet sanding. Wipe off the water and run your hand over the area—you shouldn't feel any bumps or ridges. If you do, more wet sanding is needed to feather the edges

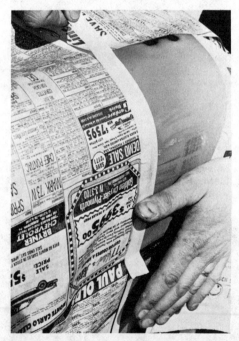

Step 6. Once you have the area sanded to your satisfaction, mask the surrounding area with masking tape and newspaper. Be sure to cover any chrome or trim that might get sprayed. You'll have to mask far enough back from the damaged area to allow for over-spray. If you mask right around the sanded spots, you'll end up with a series of lines marking the painted area

Step 7. If you haven't painted before, practice on a piece of scrap metal. Keep the can moving to avoid runs or sags. The primered areas should look like this when you have finished. It's better to spray several light coats than one heavy coat. Let the primer dry for several minutes between coats. Make sure you've covered all the bare metal

Step 8. After the primer has dried, sand the area lightly with wet 400 paper, wash it off and let it dry. Your final coat goes on next, so make sure the area is clean and dry

Step 9. Wipe the primered area dry with a clean rag and spray the finish coat of paint. Make the first coat a light coat (known as a fog coat). Keep the paint can moving smoothly 8–12 inches from the surface. Be sure to cover the area

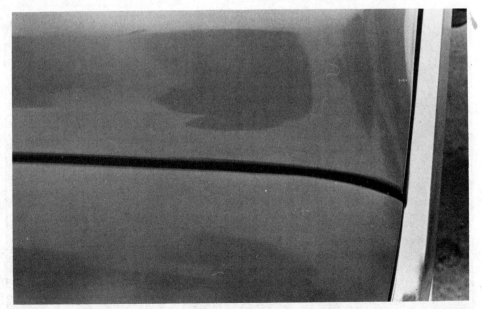

Step 10. Let the paint dry for 15 minutes before removing the masking tape. Let the paint dry for several days before rubbing it out with fine rubbing compound. This will blend the overspray into the existing paint to make the repair indistinguishable. Don't rub too hard or you'll cut through the paint

# 3

# Deep Scratches and Minor Dents

Almost every car falls prey to a deep scratch or minor dent at some time in its life. They can result from parking lot incidents, scraping the garage, vandalism or very minor accidents. These blemishes are almost always deep enough to require the use of body filler, but rarely are deep enough to pull the metal out with a puller or hammer it out from behind the panel.

This type of repair is easy to make and can save you anywhere from $50–75 at body shop prices.

## REPAIR 2

### Repairing Deep Scratches and Minor Dents

**TIME REQUIRED:** 1–1½ hours

**TOOLS**

Electric drill
Grinding attachment
Body file
Safety goggles

**MATERIALS**

*Body filler and hardener
*Sanding block
*Spreader
*80, 100, 200 and 320 sandpaper
*Primer
 Paint

*Starred items are packaged individually or in kit form by major manufacturers of auto body repair products and are available from auto supply and accessory stores.

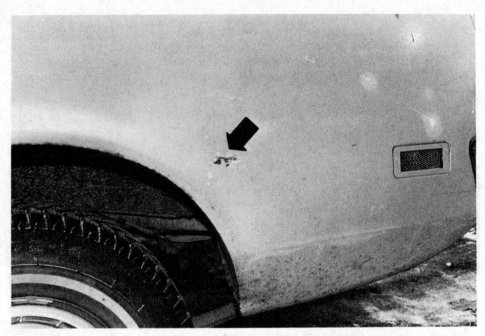

Step 1. This dent (arrow) is typical of a deep scratch or minor dent. If deep enough, the dent or scratch can be pulled out or hammered out from behind. In this case no straightening was necessary

Step 2. Using an 80-grit grinding disc on an electric drill grind the paint from the surrounding area down to bare metal. This will provide a rough surface for the body filler to grab

Step 3. The area should look like this when you're finished grinding

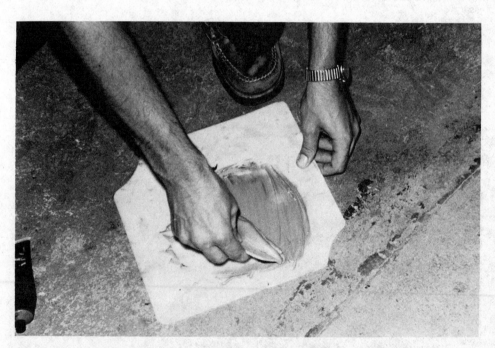

Step 4. Mix the body filler and cream hardener according to the directions

Step 5. Spread the body filler evenly over the entire area. Be sure to cover the area completely

Step 6. Let the body filler dry until the surface can just be scratched with your fingernail

Step 7. Knock the high spots from the body filler with a body file

Step 8. Check frequently with the palm of your hand for high and low spots. If you wind up with low spots, you may have to apply another layer of filler

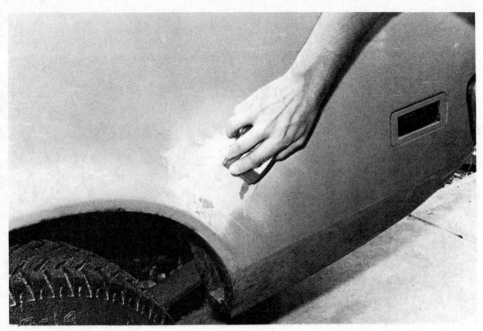

Step 9. Block sand the entire area with 320 grit paper

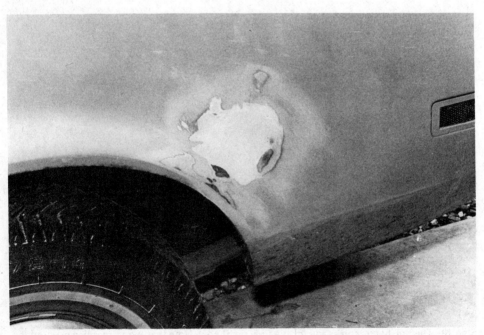

Step 10. When you're finished, the repair should look like this. Note the sand marks extending 2–3 inches out from the repaired area

Step 11. Prime the entire area with automotive primer

Step 12. The finished repair ready for the final paint coat. Note that the primer has covered the sanding marks (see Step 10). A repair of this size should be able to be spotpainted with good results. See the chapters on "Prepping for Paint" and "Painting Techniques"

# 4

## REPAIR THREE

# Small Fender Dent

This creased Volkswagen fender, is a classic parking lot dent. Careless parkers will leave you little reminders like this of their thoughtlessness. Notice that the exposed, bare metal has already begun to rust. These dents are usually too deep to simply fill in. They should be pulled out with a dent puller.

**REPAIR 3**

## Repairing Small Fender Dents

**TIME REQUIRED:** 1½–2½ hours

### TOOLS

Electric drill
Grinding attachment
Body hammer
Body file
Safety goggles

### MATERIALS

Paint paddle
*Body filler and hardener
Sanding block
*Spreader
*80, 100, 220 and 320 grit sandpaper
Squeegee
*Primer
Paint

*Starred items are packaged individually or in kit form by major manufacturers of auto body repair products and are available from auto supply and accessory stores.

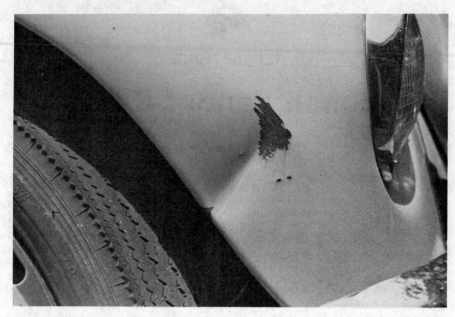

Step 1. Study the panel and read the stress lines. A little thinking here can often save a lot of work

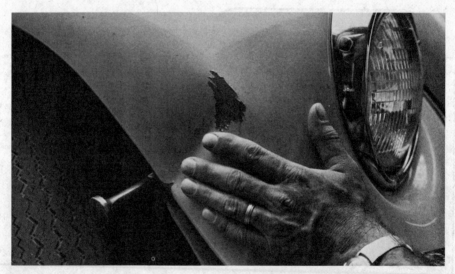

Step 2. Cautiously bump out the crease using the palm of your hand to feel your way

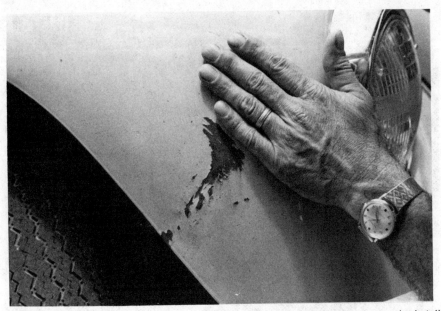

Step 3. Think straight! As you move your hand along the panel, read what your palm is telling you about the surface

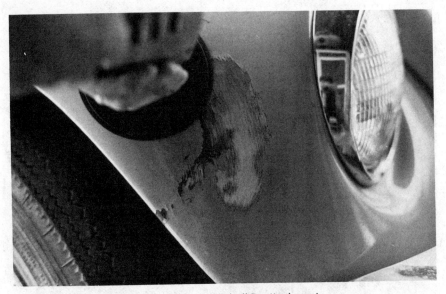

Step 4. Remove the old finish with a drill and grinding attachment

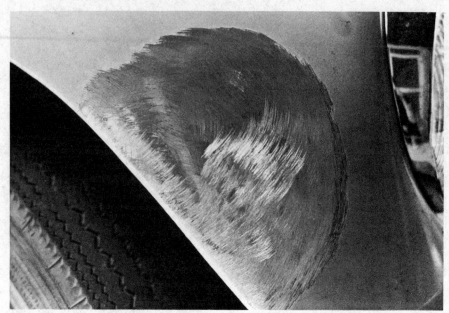

Step 5. The area should look like this when you are finished grinding

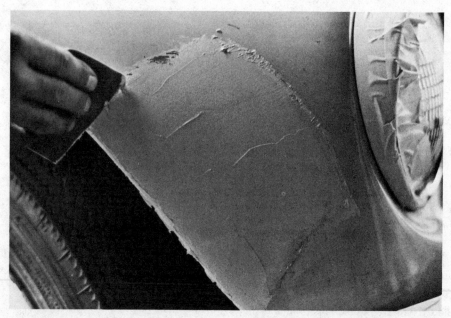

Step 6. When the panel is ground clean (above) mix the plastic (see Chapter 1) and apply plastic as quickly and as smoothly as possible (below). Mask off the chrome trim

Step 7. File the plastic before it gets too hard

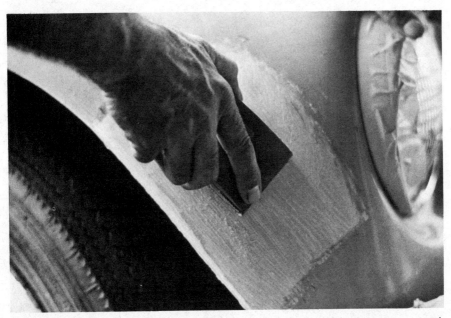

Step 8. Using a sanding block for small jobs or a sanding board for larger ones, work the plastic down to about the desired height

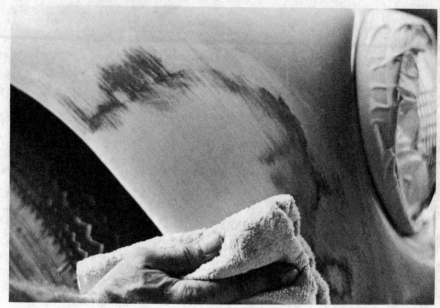

Step 9. Wipe the area with a clean rag or tack cloth

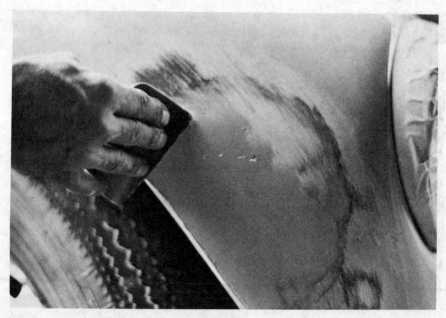

Step 10. Recoat the area with plastic body filler

Step 11. Use your file as soon as the plastic becomes solid

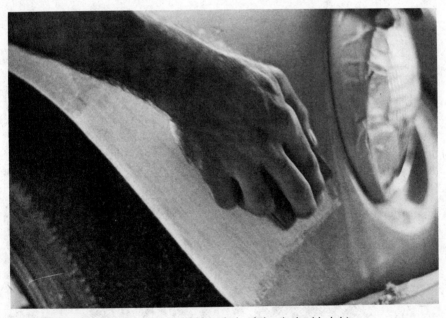

Step 12. Work the plastic down to within a hair of the desired height

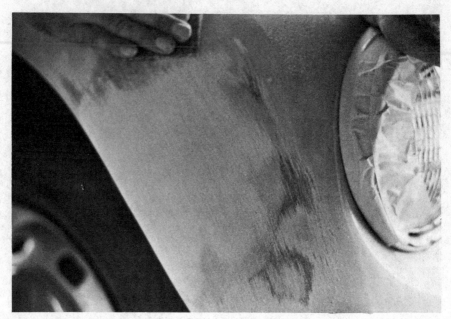

Step 13.  Finish sanding with a piece of 80-grit folded in thirds. Use long smooth strokes

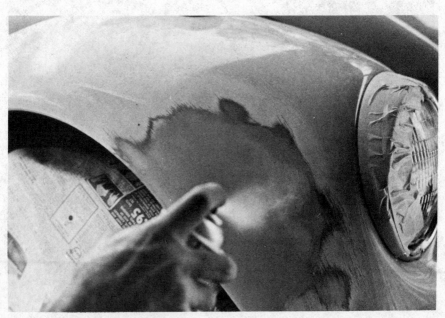

Step 14.  Prime the repair area with a medium coat

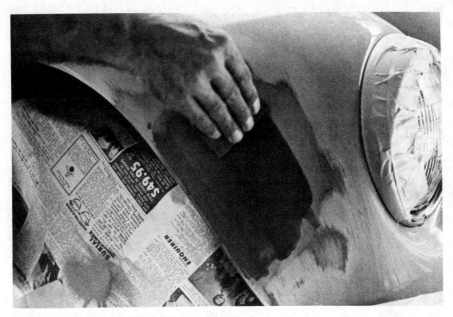

Step 15.  Apply glazing putty with a squeegee

Step 16.  After the glazing has dried, block sand with the paint paddle and 100-grit paper

Step 17.  Finish sanding with a piece of 100-grit paper folded in thirds

Step 18.  Clean the entire area with a clean rag or tack cloth

Step 19. Re-prime the entire area

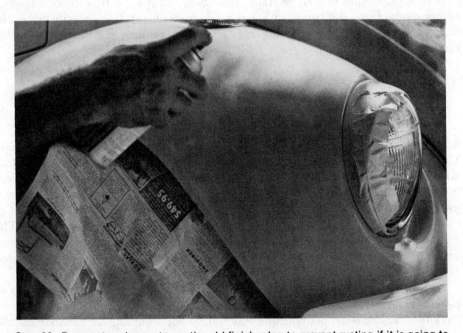

Step 20. Be sure to prime out over the old finish edge to prevent rusting if it is going to be painted later by someone else. If you are going to finish painting the panel yourself you are ready to finish sanding the primer. See the chapter on "Prepping for Paint" and "Painting Techniques"

# 5

# Rust Problems

In these days of soaring transportation costs, owners are hanging onto their cars as long as possible. Thousands of cars 10 years or older are still providing faithful service showing little or no evidence of body or structural deterioration. On the other hand, there are probably an equal number of cars and trucks taking up space in junkyards, victims of body or frame rust. Between the 2 extremes are hundreds of thousands of cars and trucks with varying degrees of rust, that not only makes the body unsightly (and possibly dangerous), but also reduces the cars value in the resale market.

## CAUSES OF RUST

Rust is an electrochemical process. It works on ferrous metals (iron and steel) from the inside out due to exposure of unprotected surfaces to air and moisture. The possibility of rust exists practically nationwide—anywhere humidity, industrial pollution or chemical salts are present, rust can form. In coastal areas, the problem is high humidity and salt air; in snowy areas, the problem is chemical salt (de-icer) used to keep the roads clear, and in industrial areas, sulpher dioxide is present in the air from industrial pollution and is changed to sulphuric acid when it rains. The rusting process is accelerated by high temperatures, especially in snowy areas, when vehicles are driven over slushy roads and then left overnight in a heated garage.

Automotive styling also can be a contributor to rust formation. Spot welding of panels creates small pockets that traps moisture and forms an environment for rust formation. Fortunately, auto manufacturers have been working hard to increase the corrosion protection of their products. Galvanized sheet metal enjoys much wider use, along with the increased use of plastic and various rust retardant coatings. Manufacturers are also designing out areas in the body where rust-forming moisture can collect.

# PREVENTING RUST

To prevent rust, you must stop it before it gets started. On new cars, there are 2 ways to accomplish this.

First, the car should be treated with a commercial rustproofing compound. There are many different brands of franchised rustproofers, but most processes involve spraying a waxy "self-healing" compound under the chassis, inside rocker panels, inside doors and fender liners and similar places where rust is likely to form. Prices for a quality rustproofing job range from $100–$250, depending on the area, the brand name and the size of the vehicle.

Ideally, the vehicle should be rustproofed as soon as possible following the purchase. The surfaces of the car or truck have begun to oxidize and deteriorate during shipping. In addition, the car may have sat on a dealer's lot or on a lot at the factory, and once the rust has progressed past the stage of light, powdery surface oxidation rustproofing is not likely to be worthwhile. Professional rustproofers feel that once rust has formed, rustproofing will simply seal in moisture already present. Most franchised rustproofing operations offer a 3–5 year warranty against rust-through, but will not support that warranty if the rustproofing is not applied within 3 months of the date of manufacture.

Undercoating should not be mistaken for rustproofing. Undercoating is a black, tar-like substance that is applied to the underside of a vehicle. Its basic function is to deaden noises that are transmitted from under the car of the areas where rust is likely to form. It simply cannot get into the crevices and seams where moisture tends to collect. In fact, it may clog up drainage holes and ventilation passages. Some under coatings also tend to crack or peel with age and only create more moisture and corrosion attracting pockets.

The second thing you should do immediately after purchasing the car is apply a paint sealout. These are petroleum based products marketed under a wide variety of brand names. It has the same protective properties as a good wax, but cover the paint with a chemically inert layer that bonds to the paint, to seal it from the air. If air can't get at it, oxidation cannot start.

The paint sealant kit consists of a base coat and conditioning coat that should be applied every 6–8 months, depending on the manufacturer. The base coat must be applied before the car is waxed, or the wax must first be removed.

Third, keep a garden hose handy for your car in winter. Use it a few times on nice days during the winter for underneath areas, and it will pay big dividends when spring arrives. Spraying under the fenders and other areas which even car-washes don't reach will help remove road salt, dirt and other build-ups which help breed rust. Adjust the nozzle to a high-force spray. An old brush will help break up residue, permitting it to be washed away more easily.

It's a somewhat messy job, but it will be worth it in the long run because a car's rust often starts in those hidden areas.

At the same time, wash grime off the door sills and, more importantly, the under portions of the doors, plus the tailgate if you have a station wagon or truck. Applying a coat of wax to those areas at least once before and once during winter will help fend off rust.

When applying the wax to the under parts of the doors, you will note small drain holes. These holes often are plugged with undercoating or dirt. Make sure they are cleaned out to prevent water build-up inside the doors. A small punch or penknife will do the job.

Water from the high-pressure sprays in carwashes sometimes can get into the housings for parking and taillights, so take a close look, and if they contain water merely loosen the retaining screws and the water should run out.

## Do-It-Yourself Rustproofing

Professional rustproofing jobs consist of drilling holes in exactly the right places through which the rustproofing is sprayed, by special equipment. Naturally, the location of the holes is different on each model, which requires precise specifications and the equipment is not inexpensive, which somewhat justifies the high price.

The alternative to a professional rustproofing job is a do-it-yourself kit, at a fraction of the cost of a professional aftermarket job. The kits consist of aerosol spray cans of rustproofing, plastic wands to reach inside panels, doors and fenders, and small rubber or plastic plugs to close the access holes that must be drilled.

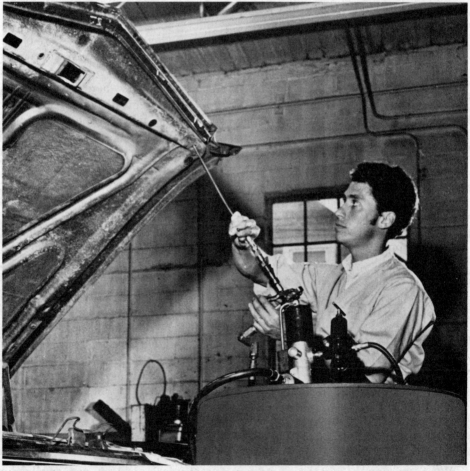

Professional rustproofing jobs are expensive, must be done within 3 months, but will protect hard to reach areas

Do-it-yourself rustproofing kits contain aerosol cans of rustproofing compound, plastic wands to reach out-of-the-way areas and rubber plugs to seal access holes

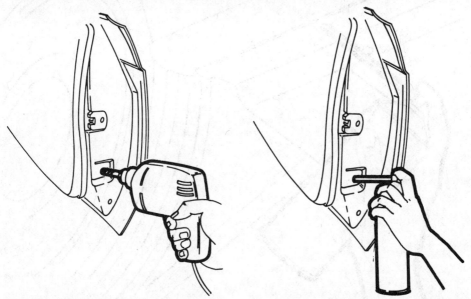

Drill a ½″ access hole in the lower half of the door. Be sure there is nothing behind the door and the windows are rolled up

Attach a wand to the spray can and insert in the door as far as possible. Coat the entire inside metal door surface

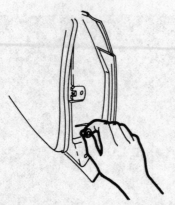

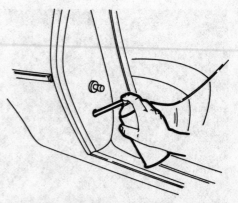

Plug the drilled hole with a ½" rubber or plastic plug. Repeat the operation for all doors and tailgates

The quarterpanel can normally be reached through the trunk or through an access hole drilled in the front part. Follow directions for the insides of doors

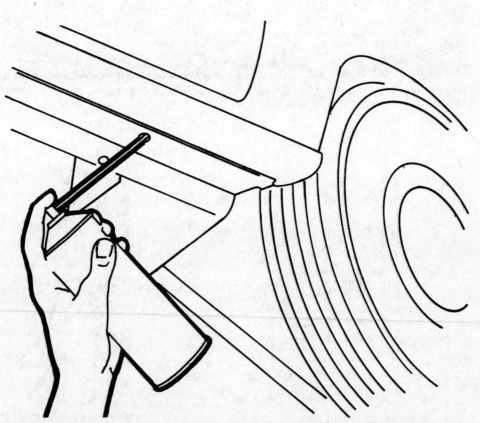

Rocker panels are one of the most rust-prone areas and access depends on the individual can. There may be drain or access holes; if not, you'll have to drill access holes

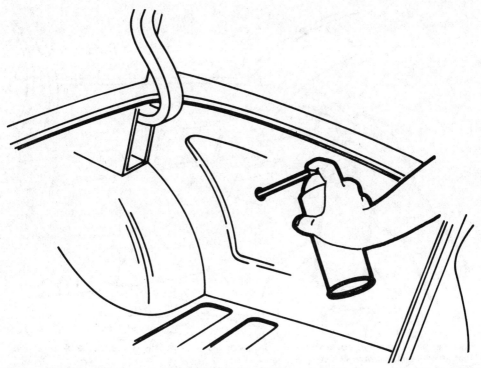

Remove the floor mats and completely clean the trunk. Spray between the rear wheelwell, floor and rear quarterpanels. Spray the bottom of the trunk and walls

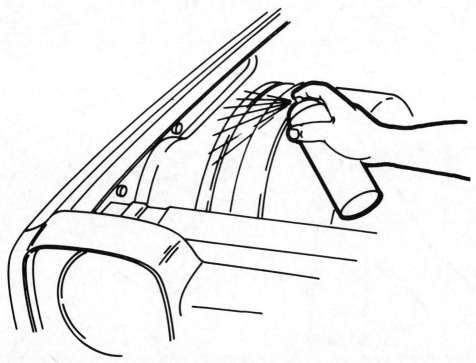

Spray all exposed areas of sheet metal, the front quarterpanel and wheel wells

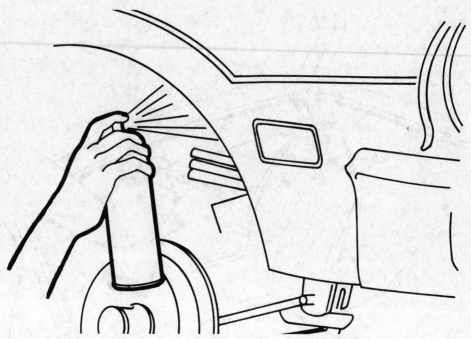

Remove the wheels and cover the brake drums or discs. Spray the entire inside of the fender liner after cleaning away all dirt

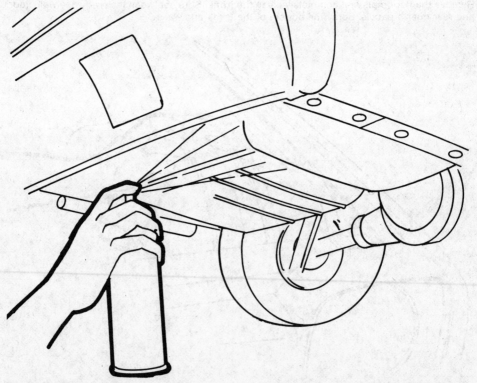

Block the wheels and support the car. Clean all loose dirt and spray the gas tank, floor pan and accessible parts of fender wells. Do not spray brake drums, drive shaft, exhaust system, shock absorbers or rubber parts

## REPAIR FOUR

# Repairing Rust Holes

Rust is the number one enemy of your car. It is the hardest problem to stop from happening and the hardest to cure once it has happened.

One thing you have to remember about rust. Even if you grind away all the rusted metal in a panel, and repair the area with any of the kits available, EVENTUALLY the rust will return. There are 2 reasons for this. One, rust is a chemical reaction that causes pressure under the repair from the inside out. That's how the blisters form. Two, the back side of the panel (and the repair) is wide open to moisture, and unpainted body filler acts like a sponge. That's why the best solution to rust problems is to remove the rusted panel and install a new one or have the rusted area cut out and a new piece of sheet metal welded in its place. The trouble with welding is the expense; sometimes it will cost more than the car is worth.

One of the better solutions to do-it-yourself rust repair is the process using a fiberglass cloth repair kit (shown here). This will give a strong repair that resists cracking and moisture and is relatively easy to use. It can be used on large or small holes and can be applied even over contoured surfaces.

## REPAIR 4

## Repairing Rust-Outs

**ESTIMATED TIME REQUIRED:** 1½–2 hours depending on size

| TOOLS | MATERIALS |
|---|---|
| Electric drill | Grinding disc (35 grit) |
| Sanding attachment | *Repair jelly |
| Scissors | *Cream hardener |
| Grease pencil or marker | *Fiberglass cloth |
| *Mixing stick | *Release film |
| *Mixing tray | *Sandpaper in 80, 100, 220 and 400 grits |
| | *Glazing compound (topcoat) |
| | *Spreaders |
| | Primer |
| | Spray paint |

*Starred items are packaged individually or in kit form by major manufacturers of auto body repair products and are available from auto supply and accessory stores.

Step 1. Rust areas such as this are common and can be easily patched

Step 2. Grind away all traces of rust with a 24-grit grinding disc. Be sure to grind back 3–4"
from the edge of the hole down to bare metal and be sure all traces of rust are removed

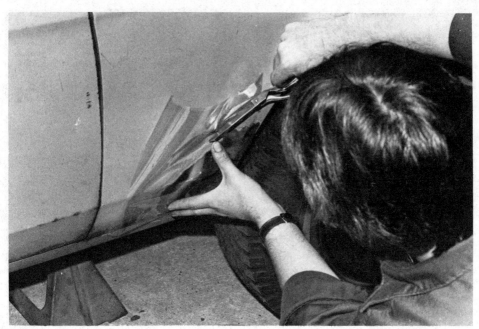

Step 3. If you are going to use the release film, cut a piece about 2″ larger than the area you have sanded. Place the film over the repair and mark the sanded area on the film. Avoid any unnecessary wrinkling of the film

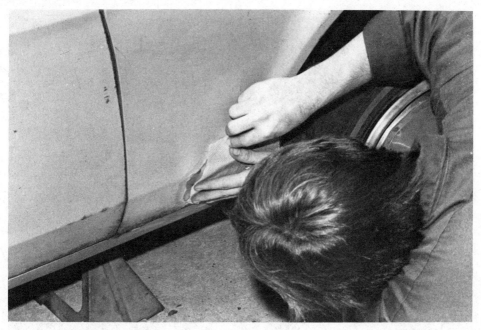

Step 4. Cut 2 pieces of fiberglass material. One piece should be about 1″ smaller than the sanded area. The second piece should be 1″ smaller than the first. Use sharp scissors to avoid loose ends

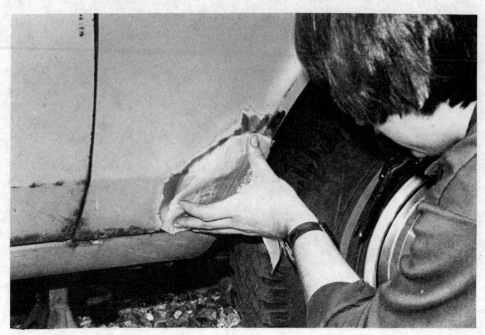

Step 5. Check the dimensions of the release film and fiberglass cloth by holding them up to the repair area

Step 6. Stir the repair jelly and place enough to saturate the fiberglass material or fill the repair area in the mixing tray. Add a 3″ ribbon of cream hardener for each ounce of repair jelly and mix until the consistency is uniform

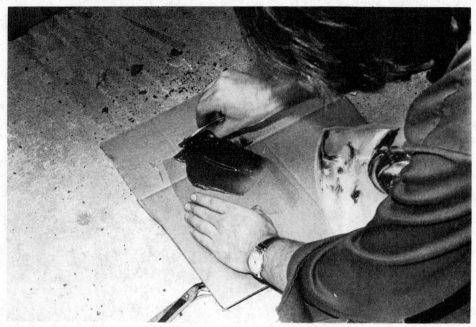

Step 7. Lay the release sheet on a flat surface and spread an even layer of filler, large enough to cover the repair

Step 8. Lay the smaller piece of fiberglass cloth in the center of the repair jelly. Spread another even coat of repair jelly larger over the fiberglass cloth and repeat the operation for the larger piece of cloth. If fiberglass material is not used, spread the repair jelly on the release film concentrated in the middle of the repair

Step 9. Place the repair material over the repair area, with the release film facing outward

Step 10. Use a spreader and work from the center outward smoothing the material, following the contours. Be sure to remove air bubbles

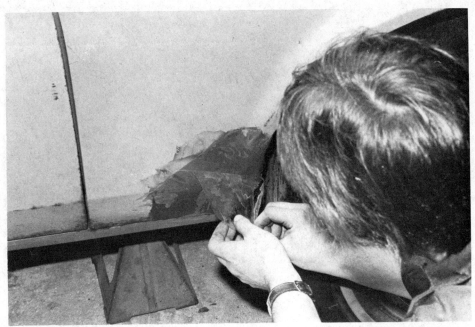

Step 11. Wait until the repair has dried tack-free and peel the release sheet off the repair. The ideal working temperature is 65°–90° F. Cooler temperatures or high humidity may require additional curing time

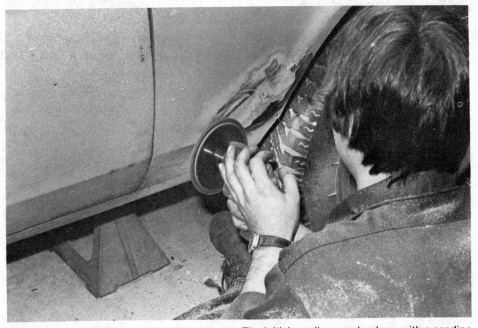

Step 12. Sand and feather-edge the entire area. The initial sanding can be done with a sanding disc

Step 13. Finish the sanding and feather-edging with a block sander

Step 14. For a smooth finish, and to prevent the glass matte from showing through, mix some topcoat with cream hardener and apply it directly with a spreader

Step 15. Sand the finish coat with finishing sandpaper

Step 16. When you're finished the repair area should look like this

Step 17.  To finish this repair, grind out the surface rust along the top edge of the rocker panel

Step 18.  Mix some more repair jelly and cream hardener (see Step 6) and apply it directly over the surface. When it dries tack-free, block sand the surface smooth

Step 19. Sand the repair. When finished the whole repair should look like this. Note the taped door edge preparatory to painting

Step 20. Spray the entire area with a primer coat

Step 21. The repair is now ready to be painted with a finish coat. See the Chapters on "Prepping for Paint" and "Painting Techniques"

# 6

## REPAIR FIVE

# Creased Panel and
# Door Edge

This little crease in the Volkswagen's door is easily repaired using a dent puller. This 17 step procedure will restore the car's beauty and value at a fraction of the cost to have it repaired in a body shop.

## REPAIR 5

### Repairing a Creased Panel

**TIME REQUIRED:** 1–1½ hours

#### TOOLS

Electric drill
Grinding attachment
Drill bit (½ size of end of the dent
   puller)
Body file
Sanding block
Safety goggles

#### MATERIALS

*Plastic body filler and hardener
*Glazing putty
  Clean cloths or tack rag
  Paint paddle
*Sanding paper in 80, 100, 220 and
   320 grits depending on whether
   you're going to paint it yourself
*Primer
  Paint
  Squeegee
*Spreader

*Starred items are packaged individually or in kit form by major manufacturers of auto body repair products and are available from auto supply and accessory stores.

Step 1. Evaluate the damage. There is no way to tap this out from the inside, so it will have to be pulled out with a dent puller

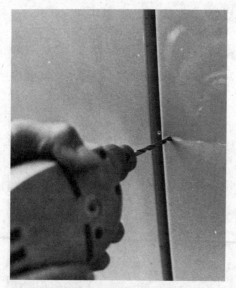

Step 2. Drill holes along the stress line

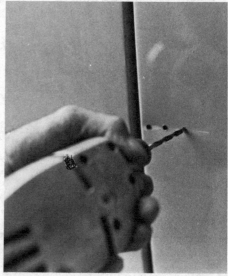

Step 3. Holes should be spaced one inch apart

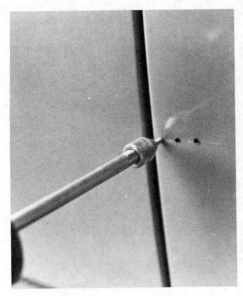

Step 4. Use the dent puller to bring the panel back to its original shape

Step 5. Several light taps in each hole will keep the panel even. If it is still too low, re-peat the step

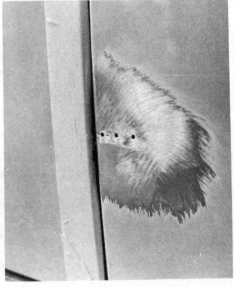

Step 6. Mask the door edge and grind the old finish back

Step 7. After grinding the area should look like this

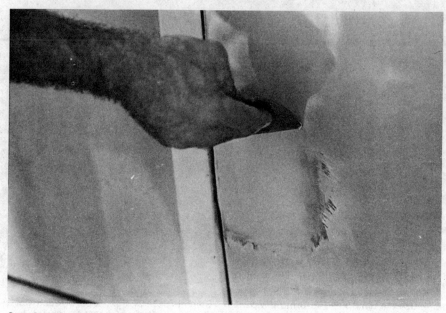

Step 8. Mix and apply the first coat of filler using a spreader

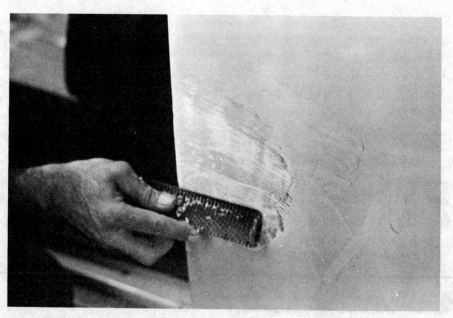

Step 9. File off any high spots as soon as the plastic becomes solid

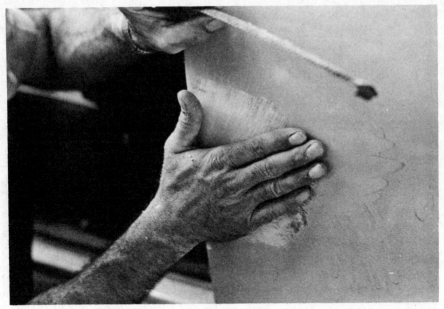

Step 10.  Think straight. Find the highs and lows with your most valuable tool—the hand

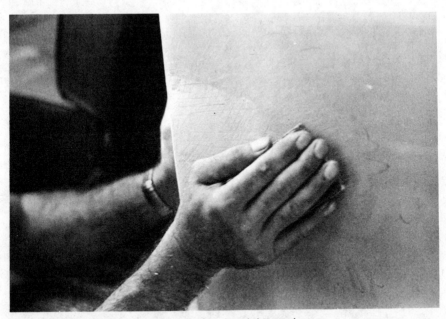

Step 11.  Feel the high spots with your hand and the sandpaper

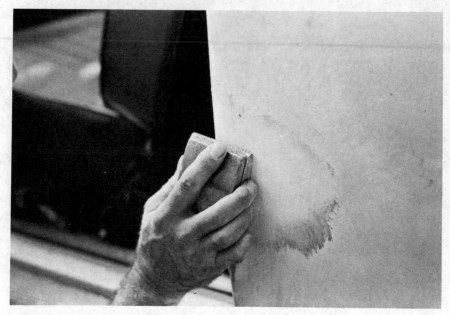

Step 12. Work the plastic down with the appropriate sanding tool

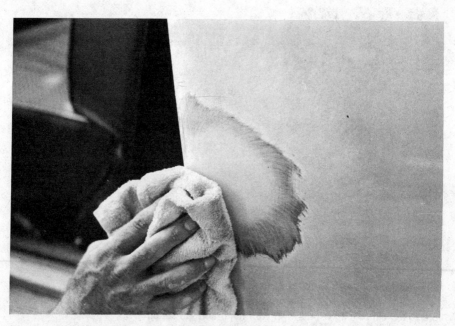

Step 13. Wipe the repair area clean with a rag

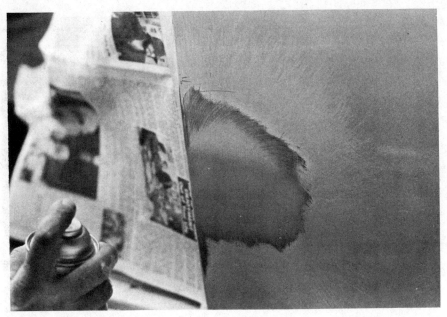

Step 14. Mask the area and prime it with a medium coat

Step 15. Apply the glazing putty with a squeegee

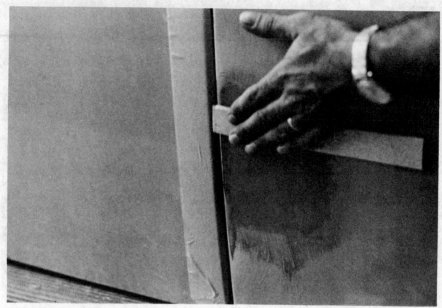

Step 16. Block sand the area with 100-grit paper wrapped around a paint paddle

Step 17. Prime the entire area. You are now ready to finish sand and paint the area. See the chapters on "Prepping for Paint" and "Painting Techniques"

# 7

## REPAIRS SIX AND SEVEN

# Dented Trunk Lid or Hood

The following two repairs differ only in that the panels are functional. The hood and the trunk lid, or deck lid as it is sometimes called, must open and close properly, so in addition to straightening the sheet metal, you have to align the panel so that it fits squarely in the opening it covers. This is not difficult, but will take some time and adjustment to get it right. As in the previous jobs, take your time and think the problem out.

## REPAIR 6 AND 7

## Repairing a Dented Trunk or Hood

**TIME REQUIRED:** 2–3 hours each

### TOOLS

Electric drill
Drill bit (½ size of end of dent puller)
Grinding attachment for electric drill
Dent puller
Open end adjustable wrench
Screwdriver
Socket wrench
Body file
Safety goggles

### MATERIALS

*Plastic body filler and hardener
*Glazing putty
Clean cloths
Paint paddle
Sanding block
*Sanding paper in 28, 80, 100, 220 and 400 grits
Block of wood
*Primer and paint
*Spreader

*Starred items are packaged individually or in kit form by major manufacturers of auto body repair products and are available from auto supply and accessory stores.

Whenever you are working on a hood panel or deck lid, follow these basic steps.

1. Straighten the dent or damage that has been done to the panel by pulling or knocking it out as described in other repairs.

2. When the dent is roughed out and *before* you apply the plastic filler, align the panel so it fits the opening properly. There are several adjustments that can be made here. Though they seem impossible at first, take your time and follow the step-by-step photos.

3. When you have the dent roughed out and the panel aligned properly in the opening, apply your filler as you did before. The only other difference with these panels (hoods and trunk lids) is that they are very visible to anyone looking at or driving the car. So do an extra special job so that your work is sure not to show. The best compliment any body man can be paid is for someone to say, "You can never notice his work."

One word of caution here for safety's sake. Upon repairing the hood panel, check the hood latch assembly. If there is any damage or if the latch doesn't seem to work well, go to the dealer and buy a new unit. Many a hood latch has been repaired just enough to get by only to have the hood fly open at high speed, creating all kinds of havoc. Don't take the chance to save the low price or a new latch assembly.

The same problem exists with the trunk latch assembly. It is not likely to become a life and death situation, but if you try to repair a trunk latch that should really be replaced, you may find yourself unable to get into your trunk. This could be really frustrating after a thirty-mile drive to your favorite fishing spot when you find you can't get to your fishing gear on the inside. *Replace latches that appear to be bad.*

## REPAIRING A DENTED TRUNK LID

This trunk lid was hit just above the bumper. Follow the proper steps in repairing it. Pull out the dent, align the lid in the opening and metal finish the dent

Arrow shows how the impact knocked the lid out of alignment

The same deck lid at another angle. Note the trunk lid-body seam (arrows). The lid is pushed up at the upper arrow. When properly aligned, the gap in this seam will be even

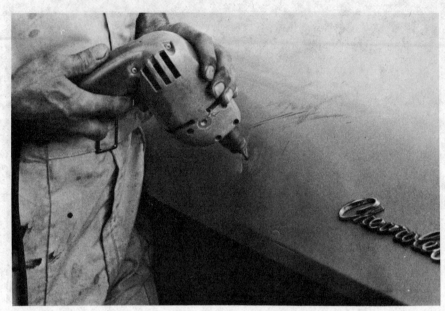

Step 1. Before attempting to align the lid, rough out the dent. This will remove any unseen stress in the lid. Make your holes for the puller with a drill. It may be possible to push the dent out from inside. See Crumpled Rear Quarterpanel

Step 2. Bring the lid panel back to its original position with the puller

Step 3. Grind back the old finish, using an electric drill and grinding attachment with 28 grade paper

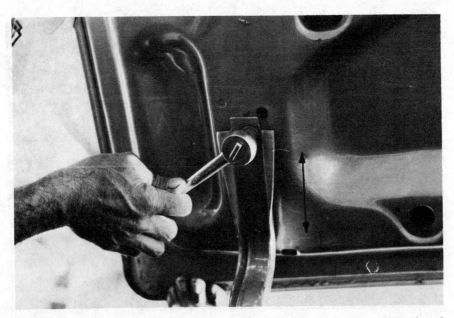

Step 4. Before applying plastic filler, align the lid in the opening. Arrows show the adjustment direction

Step 5. After the lid is properly aligned, the gap in the seams will be even. Continue making minor adjustments until the gap is even all the way around

Step 6. In cases where the leading edge of the lid is too high or too low, you will have to bend the hinges. To lower the leading edge (front of lid), simply open the trunk lid fully and then force it up

Step 7. To raise the leading edge of the trunk lid, use a wooden block as shown and force the lid down. Do one side at a time. The hinge will bend at the arrow

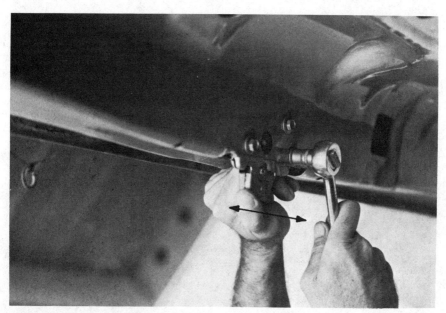

Step 8. To raise or lower the rear edge of the lid, simply adjust the latch mechanism. On this model, the latch assembly is in the lid and adjusts from side to side. The striker is on the rear body panel. The arrows show direction of adjustment

Step 9.  On some cars, the adjustment locations are reversed from those shown in Step 8

Step 10.  Mix and apply the body filler. When it has dried sufficiently, cut it down with a body file (cheese grater)

Step 11.  When the high spots have been removed with the body file, work it down with a block sander and 100 grit paper

Step 12.  Apply another coat

Step 13. Block sand the plastic with a rubber block or sanding board

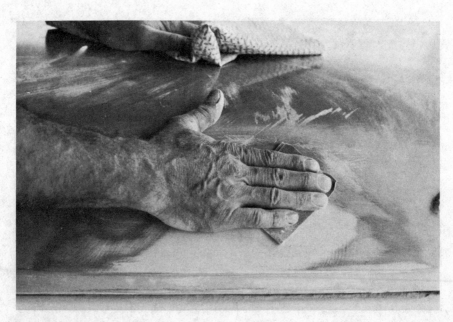

Step 14. Just before priming, sand the area smooth with a piece of 100-grit in the palm of the hand

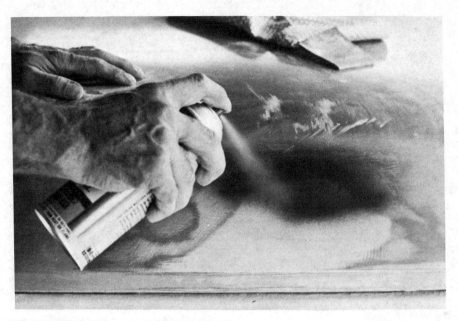

Step 15. Prime the area as in other repairs

After the primer dries, coat the area with glazing putty

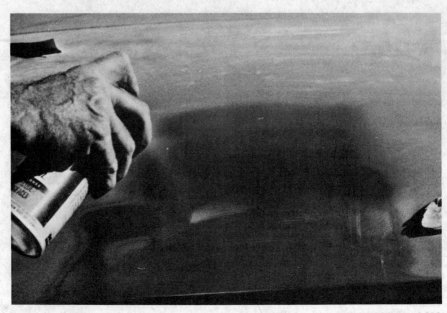

Step 17. After the putty dries and you have block sanded it with a paint paddle and 220-grit paper, prime the entire area and prepare it for painting

# REPAIRING A DENTED HOOD PANEL

This repair involves the hood panel. This panel was hit in the right front knocking it out of alignment on the left side

The same basic procedures will be used to make this repair as were used to repair the dented trunk lid

Step 1. Drill holes for the dent puller at the stress line(s)

Step 2. Straighten the dent by pulling it out with the dent puller. It may be possible to push the dent out from behind (see Crumpled Rear Quarterpanel)

Step 3. Grind the old finish back

Step 4. Before you apply any plastic, align the hood in the opening. There are usually four bolts on each hinge. The two bolts holding the hood to the hinge adjust the hood forward and back. The two bolts that hold the hinge to the fender control the height of the rear edge of the hood. See the chapter on aligning body panels for illustrations and more details

Step 5. Once the hood is properly aligned, the hood-fender seams should look like this. Note that the gaps are equal on both sides and are level with the fender panels

Step 6. Hood height is adjusted as shown. Turn the lock shaft clockwise to lower the front of the hood. Turn counterclockwise to raise the front of the hood

Step 7. Be sure the hood latch is operating properly. A bad hood latch is dangerous. When the hood is fitting and operating properly, you can metal finish the damaged area as in the previous repair ("Repairing a Dented Trunk Lid") and be ready to paint

# 8

## REPAIR EIGHT

# Crumpled Rear Quarter Panel

At first glance, this damaged Oldsmobile Toronado rear quarterpanel looks like a job that belongs in a body shop. However, you can repair this panel yourself with patience and careful attention to these instructions.

This job would cost several hundred dollars to have it repaired professionally. All it will cost you is these tools, materials and your time.

## REPAIR 8

### Repairing a Crumpled Rear Quarter Panel

**TIME REQUIRED:** 4–6 hours

**TOOLS**

Hammer
Body hammer
Block of wood
Yardstick
Electric drill
Grinding attachment
Body file
Sanding board and block
Safety goggles

**MATERIALS**

*Plastic body filler and hardener
*Glazing putty
 Rag or tack cloth
 Paint paddle
*Spreader
 Squeegee
*Sandpaper in 36, 80, 100, 220 and
    320 grits depending on whether
    you're going to paint it yourself
*Primer
 Paint

*Starred items are packaged individually or in kit form by major manufacturers of auto body repair products and are available from auto supply and accessory stores.

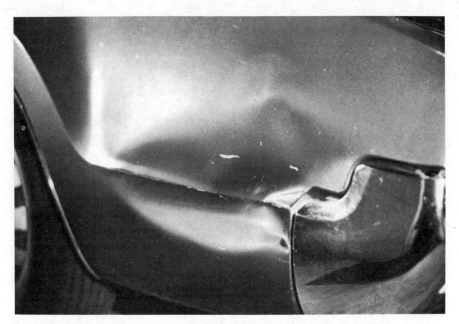

This job looks bad, but can be repaired if you think it out and proceed slowly

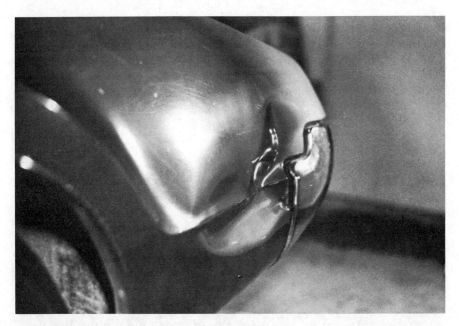

Step 1. Study the damage. Look at the other side of the car and study the lines of the undamaged panel

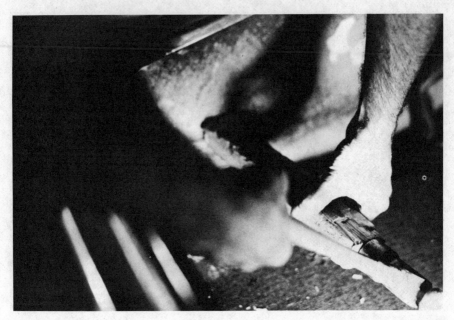

Step 2. Return the panel to its original position by tapping it out with a block of wood and a hammer

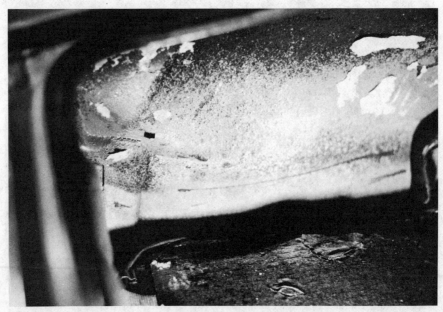

Step 3. This job was easier because access to the back side of the panel was possible through the trunk

Step 4. Shape the panel. When a panel is hit this hard, you have low areas (small dents) and high spots (arrows)

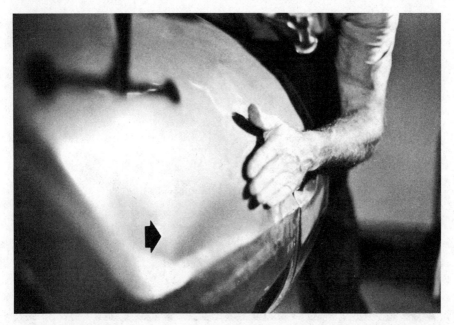

Step 5. Work the high spots down as you bring the panel back to its original shape

Step 6.  On large areas like this, use a yardstick to locate highs and lows and check body lines

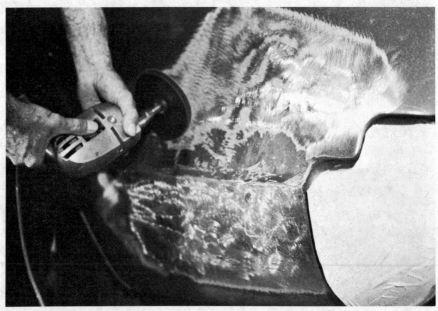

Step 7.  Grind off the old finish. After grinding, you may find small areas that are still not right. Correct them now

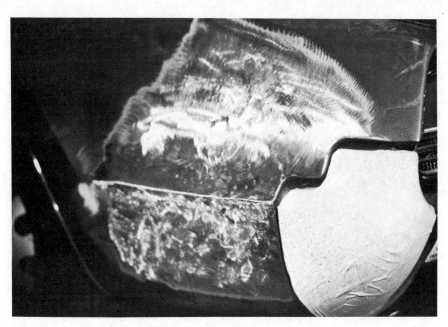

Step 8. Correct the high spots. When you are finished shaping and grinding the area should look like this. Compare the shape to the undamaged side

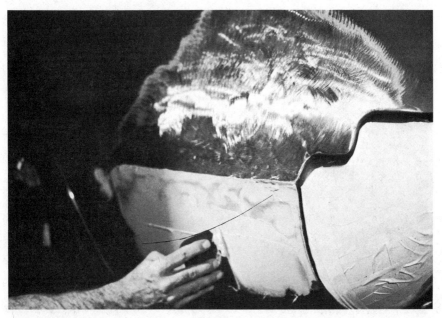

Step 9. With the finish ground back (above) tin the metal with small amounts of plastic on a spreader (below)

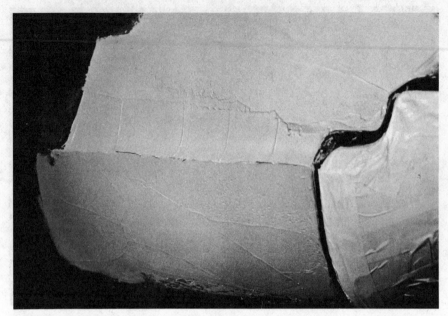

Step 10. Spread the plastic as smoothly as possible

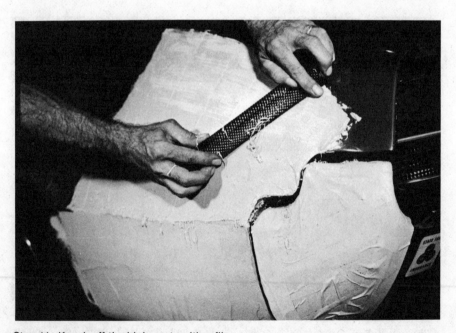

Step 11. Knock off the high spots with a file

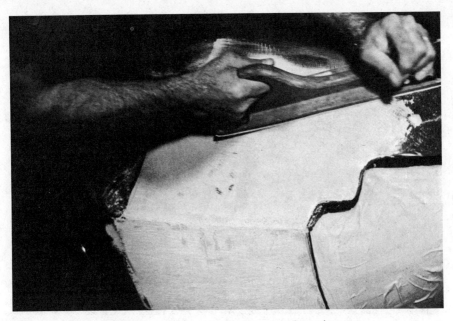

Step 12.  Work the plastic down with a sanding board and rough paper

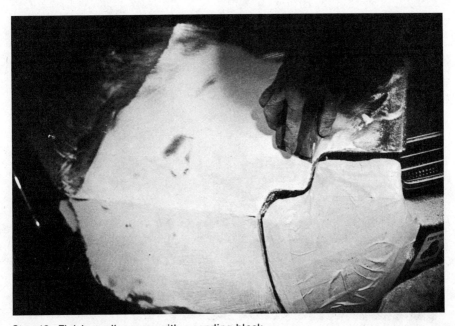

Step 13.  Finish smaller areas with a sanding block

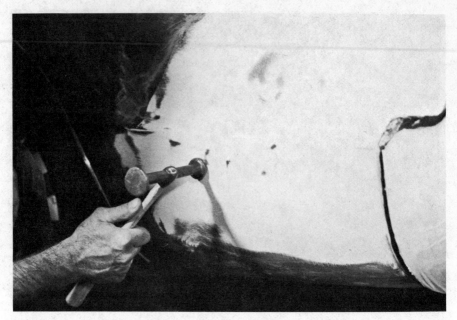

Step 14. High spots in the metal will become apparent as you sand. These can be tapped down with a body hammer before the next coat of filler is applied

Step 15. On a curve such as this body line, a piece of 17 in. x 2⅔ in. (36-grit) sandpaper rolled into a tube shape does a great job

Step 16. Use the yardstick to be sure the lines are shaping up correctly and to show high and low spots. Run your hand over the area to visualize the low and high spots

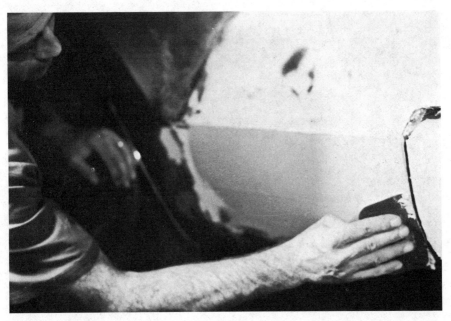

Step 17. Recoat the area with body filler. Keep the low areas in mind when applying the filler

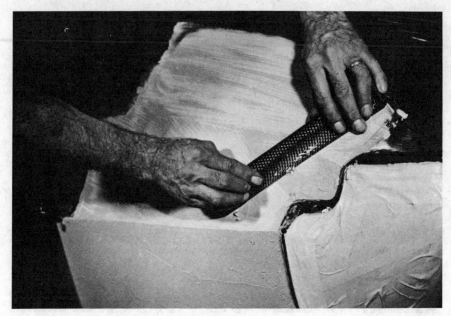

Step 18. Knock off any high spots with the file

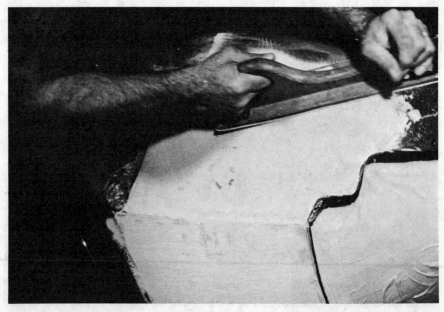

Step 19. Work the plastic down with sanding board and block. If a third and fourth application are needed, don't feel bad

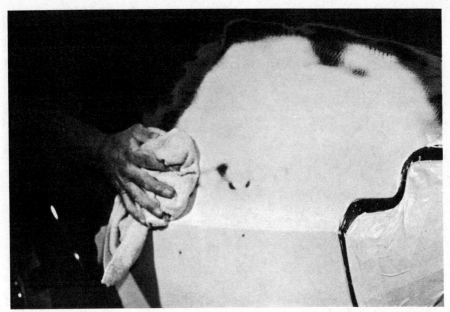

Step 20. When you have the desired surface wipe it clean with a rag or tack cloth

Step 21. Mask and prime the area with a medium coat of primer (below)

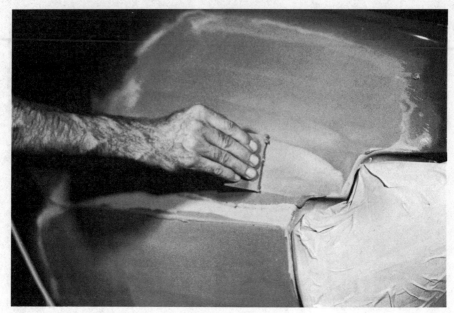

Step 22. Glaze the area in one-stroke applications

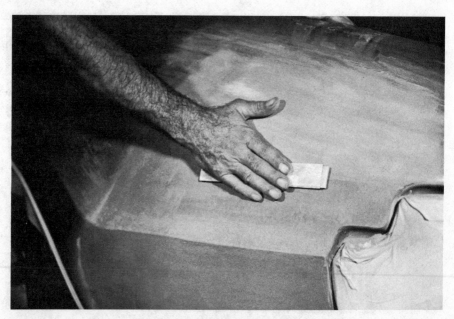

Step 23. When dry, block sand the area with 100-grit sand paper wrapped around a paint paddle

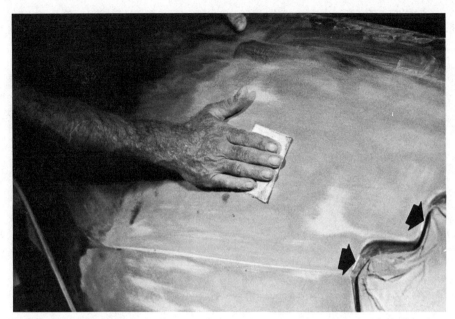

Step 24. Finish sand with 100-grit folded in thirds. Use long, light, even strokes. Be sure edges are straight, and don't allow excess material to build up (arrows)

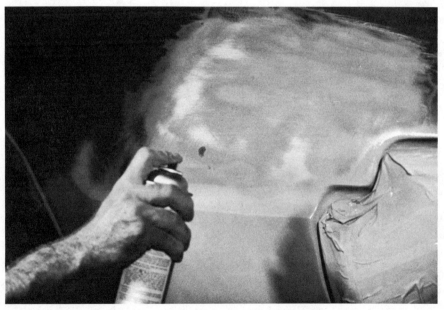

Step 25. Prime the entire area, being sure that all bare metal is covered

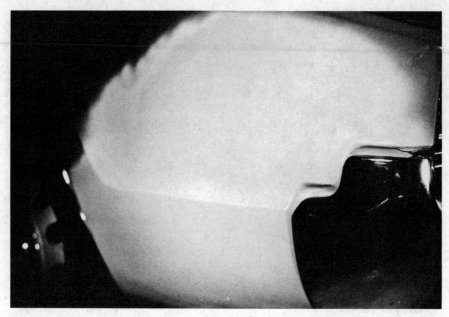

Step 26. The finished product ready for paint. See the chapters on "Prepping for Paint" and "Painting Techniques"

# 9

## REPAIR NINE

# Damaged Door and Front Quarter Panel

This Dodge Dart was a victim of overnight street parking. This is a typical gouge or dent that must be repaired using a dent puller and body filler techniques. Most of the work involved with this repair is returning the panel to its original shape. Work slowly and use the other side as a guide.

## REPAIR 9

### Repairing a Damaged Door and Front Quarterpanel

**TIME REQUIRED:** 5–7 hours

**TOOLS**

Electric drill
Drill bit
Dent puller and body hook (if necessary)
Screwdriver
Grinding attachment for electric drill
Wire brush attachment for electric drill
Body file
Sanding block or board
Safety goggles

**MATERIALS**

Body molding adhesive
Clean clothes
*Sanding paper 28, 80, 100, 220, 320 and 400 grits
*Body putty and hardener
*Spreaders
*Glazing putty
*Primer
Paint

*Starred items are packaged individually or in kit form by major manufacturers of auto body repair products and are available from auto supply and accessory stores.

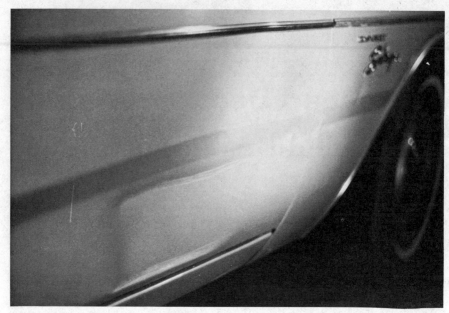

This is a typical gauge, but with a little patience you can easily do it at home

Step 1. Study the stress lines, and drill the holes for the dent puller

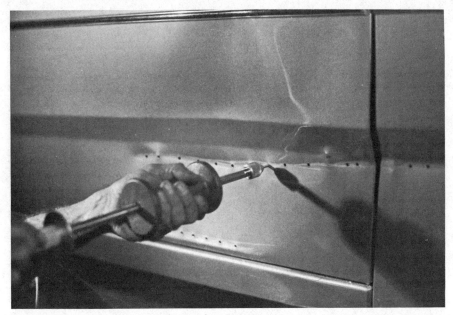

Step 2. Gradually work the panel back into position. As you are using the dent puller, watch what the rest of the panel is doing

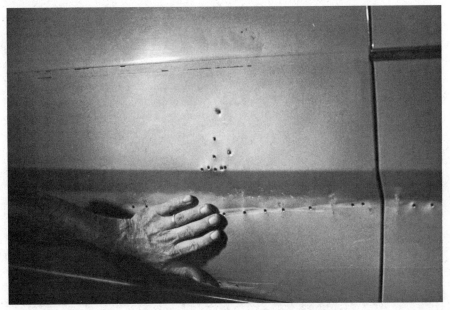

Step 3. Use the palm of your hand to find highs and lows. Work them out as smooth as possible as you go

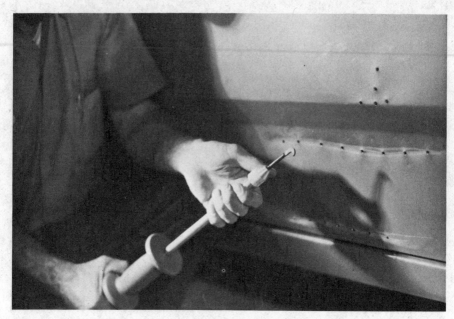

Step 4. This body hook tool is very handy and comes with some dent pullers. It is used when you can get behind the edge of the damaged panel

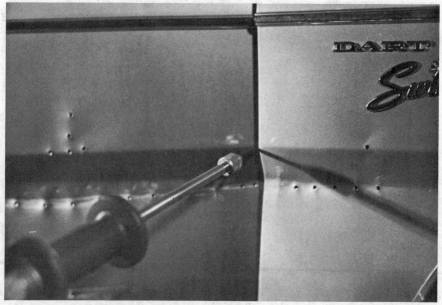

Step 5. The edge of this fender is easily brought out to the proper position with the body hook

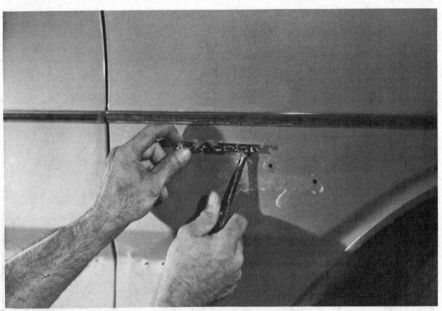

Step 6. Most emblems are fastened to the body by means of barrel type fasteners. They are easily removed with a small screwdriver, but be careful you don't break the emblem

Step 7. This is the latest type of side molding. It is easily replaced with a good trim adhesive

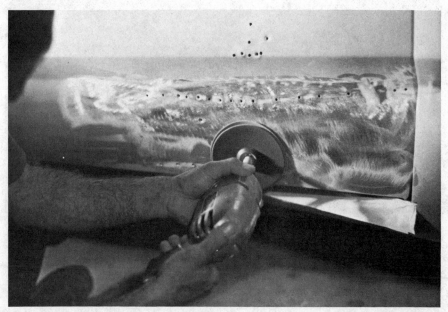

Step 8. Begin the grinding operation when you are sure the panel is as close to the original as you can get it. Use a 28 or 35 grit grinding disc

Step 9. Grind the old finish well back from the damage. Notice that one panel at a time is finished

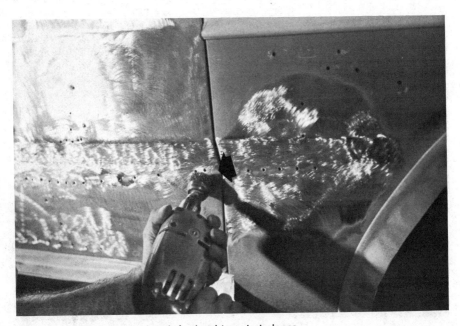

Step 10. Use a small wire brush for hard-to-get-at places

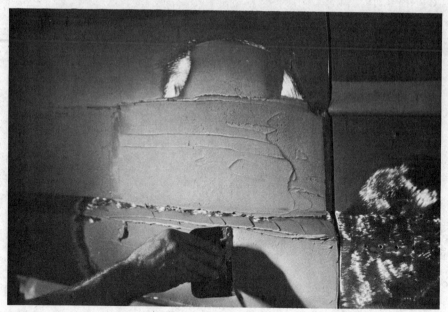

Step 11. Mix the plastic and spread it as smoothly and quickly as possible. On panels with sculptured lines such as this, concentrate on those lines first. Then do the low spots on the flat portions of the panel

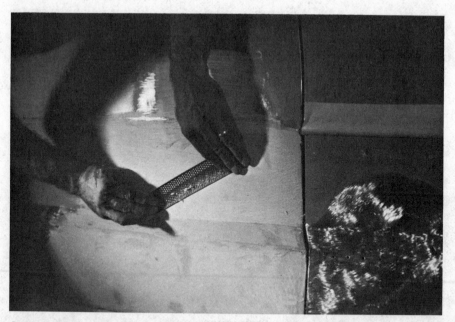

Step 12. Work the plastic down with a file as soon as it becomes solid. Notice that only one panel at a time is finished. This way the plastic doesn't get too hard on one panel while you are working on the other

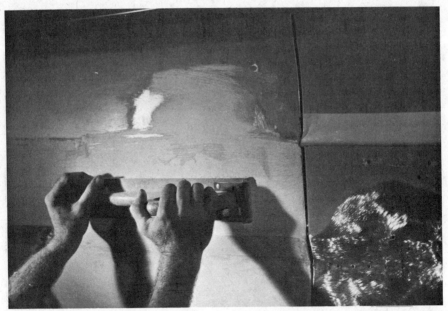

Step 13. Use a sanding board with 80 and 100 grit paper on large areas like this to obtain straight panels

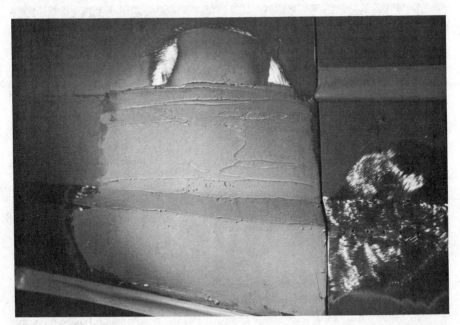

Step 14. Recoat the panel as many times as necessary to obtain smooth contours

Step 15. After the first panel is done, start on the second

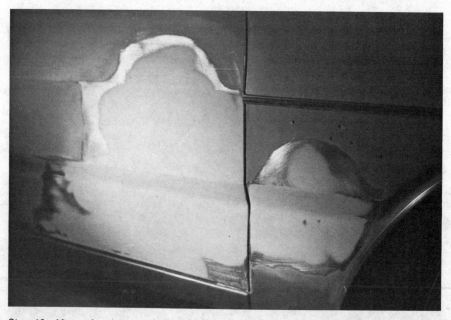

Step 16. After a few hours your panels should look like this. Prime and glaze as in the previous repairs, and you're ready for paint. When a large surface is involved it's probably better to paint the entire panel and door rather than try to match the paint and blend it in

# 10

## REPAIR TEN

# Repairing Fiberglass Panels

Many panels on today's cars are made of fiberglass to reduce weight and resist the elements. The front nosepiece, the rear quarterpanel extensions spoiler and smaller panels are frequent places to encounter fiberglass. The crack in the fender of this early Corvette and the procedures used to make the repair are also typical of any fiberglass body panel.

NOTE: *Many people are allergic to the fiberglass dust produced by sanding. Be sure to work in a well-ventilated area, wear a protective dust mask and clothing that covers your arms and legs.*

## REPAIR 10

### Repairing Fiberglass Panels

**TIME REQUIRED:** 2–3 hours

#### TOOLS

Electric drill
Grinding attachment for electric
  drill
Body file
Protective dust mask
Safety goggles

#### MATERIALS

* Polyester resin
* Hardener
* Spreader
* Fiberglass mat (cloth)
  Sandpaper in 80, 100, 220 and 400
    grit
  Grinding disc (35 grit)
* Plastic filler and hardener
* Body putty

*Starred items are packaged individually or in kit form by major manufacturers of auto body repair products and are available from auto supply and accessory stores.

Step 1. The crack in the fiberglass panel of this '59 Corvette is typical of the repair to almost any fiberglass panel

Step 2. Use an 80 grit grinding disc on an electric drill and grind the paint down to bare fiberglass. Use the edge of the grinding disc to remove all loose material from the crack

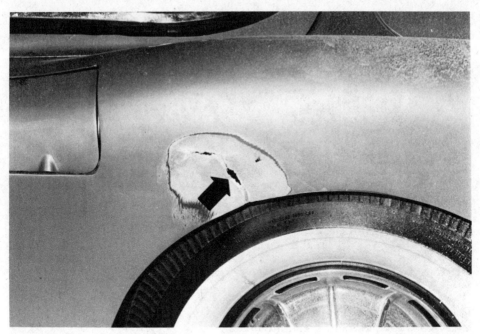

Step 3. When you've finished, the area should look like this. Notice that the edges of the crack have been leveled inward to form a "V" for better adhesion

Step 4. Use scissors to cut a piece of fiberglass cloth to roughly the shape of the sanded area (no larger). For more strength, depending on the size of the crack, you can also cut a smaller piece of cloth to fill the crack

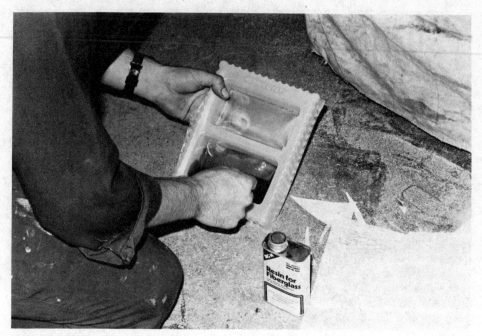

Step 5.  Follow the directions and mix the resin and hardener

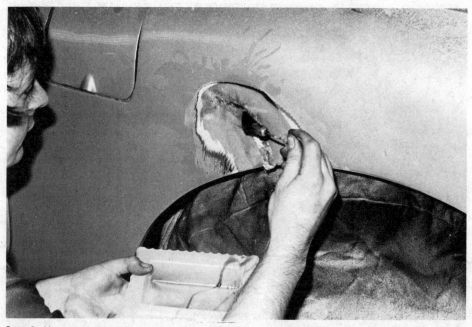

Step 6.  Use a small brush and coat the crack and surrounding area with the resin. Be sure the resin coats the area where the patch will be applied

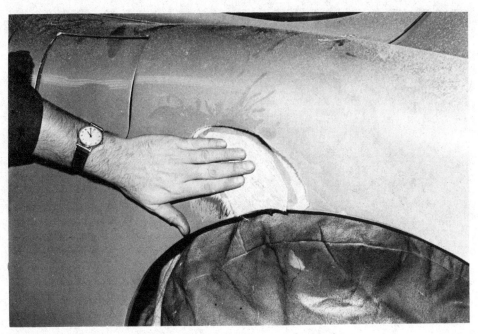

Step 7. Lay the piece(s) of fiberglass cloth in place over the crack

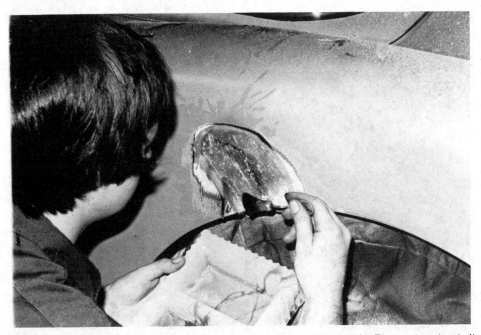

Step 8. Use a small brush and saturate the fiberglass cloth with the resin. Be sure to saturate it thoroughly and cover the edges of the fiberglass cloth

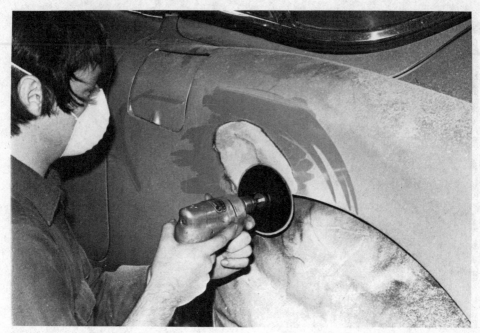

Step 9. Allow the repair to dry thoroughly. Using the electric drill and a medium grit sanding disc, sand the entire repair area

Step 10. When you're finished, the area should look like this. Check with your hand for high or low spots. Minor bubbles in the cloth can be sanded away and filled later

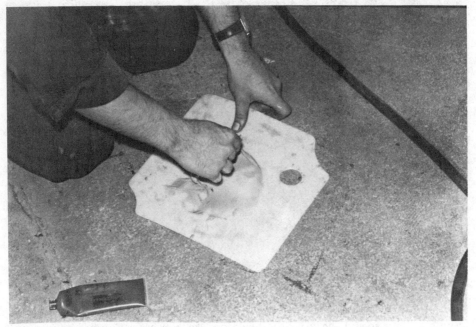

Step 11. Mix some plastic body filler, following the directions on the container

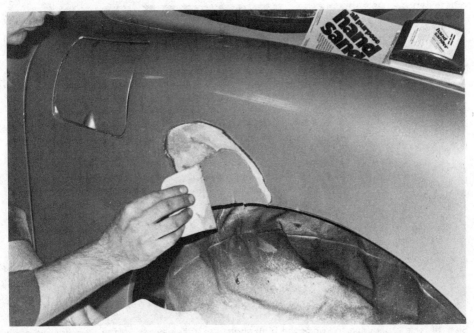

Step 12. Apply the body filler using a medium size spreader. Apply the filler in long, even strokes, making sure you cover the entire sanded area

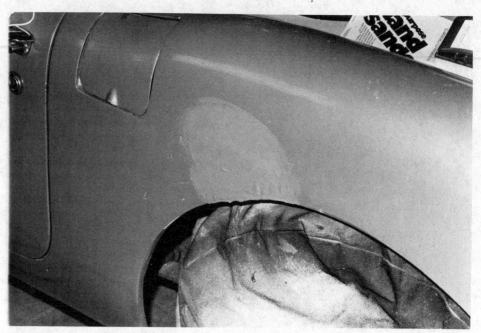

Step 13. Properly applied, the body filler should look like this when you've finished applying it. Allow the filler to dry until you can nick the surface with a fingernail

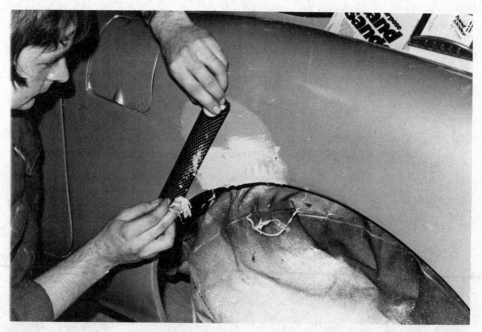

Step 14. Use a body file to knock the high spots, you may have to let the filler dry and apply another coat of filler, and cut it down with the file again

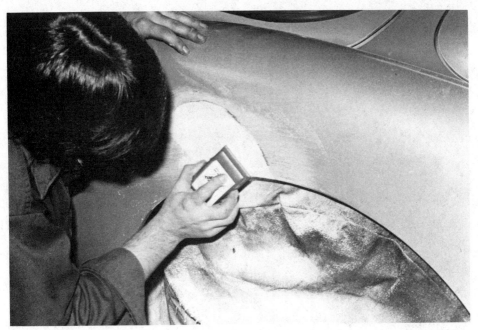

Step 15. Using a sanding block and medium grit paper, block sand the entire area smooth

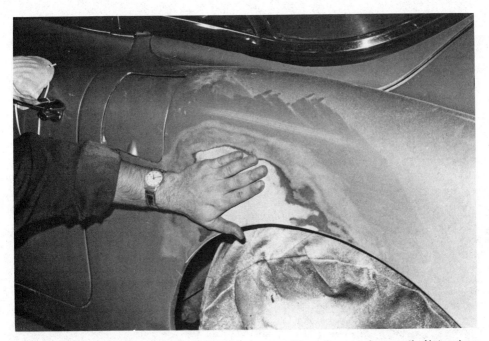

Step 16. Check with the palm of your hand to be sure the entire area is smooth. Note where the sand marks extend well beyond the repair area to be sure the edges are feather-edged

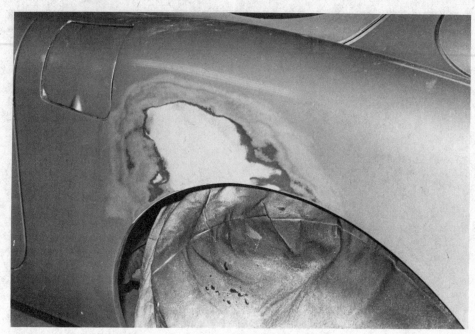

Step 17. When you're ready for primer, the entire area should look like this

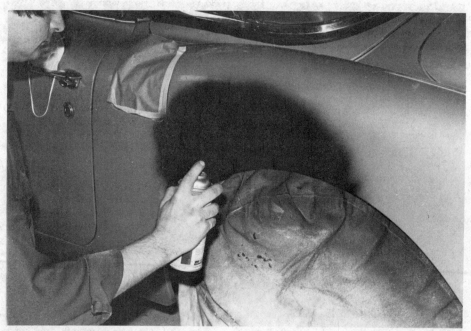

Step 18. Mask off any chrome or trim pieces adjacent to the repair and prime the entire area

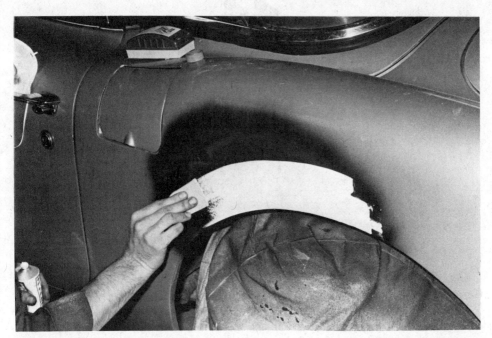

Step 19. When the primer is dry, apply glazing putty over the primed area. The glazing putty is applied direct from the container to fill in minor surface imperfections. It should be applied in long, even strokes, using just enough putty for a light coat. Try not to go over areas where you have already applied putty. When you've finished the area is ready for final sanding with 400 grit paper, in preparation for paint. This particular paint job was left to a body shop because (1) the car was silver, one of the most difficult colors to spray and match and (2) the entire panel was to be repainted for as close a match as possible

# 11

## REPAIR ELEVEN

# Vinyl Top Repairs

Your car's vinyl top is extremely decorative and vulnerable to damage. The vinyl fabric can be torn, cut or cracked either from abuse or neglect.

To have a new vinyl top put on your car is an expensive proposition, running well over $100.00. Fortunately, if the damage is small, it can be repaired using repair and resoration products especially for vinyl tops.

The procedure shown here is basically the one used by major car manufacturers, and can produce an almost invisible repair. They key to the process however, is the "Micro-Heat Beam® curing tool", which although inexpensive (about $15) is currently available only from the manufacturer, Repair-It Industries, Inc. A household iron or other type of heating device will burn or overheat the surrounding area, resulting in an unsatisfactory repair. The other repair materials can be purchased separately.

---

### REPAIR 11

### Repairing a Vinyl Top

**TIME REQUIRED:** ½–1 hour depending on size of repair

**TOOLS**

Razor blade
Thin bladed spatula
*Heat curing tool (see above)

**MATERIALS**

*Backing fabric
*Graining paper
*Vinyl repair compound
Vinyl Top dressing

*Starred items are available in kit form directly from the manufacturer. All items except the heating tool are also available locally.

Step 1. Assess the damage. This small tear is typical of minor vinyl top damage

Step 2. Clean the damaged area and remove any loose threads with a razor blade or razor knife. Trim the damage neatly using the same razor blade or knife. Cut a piece of the backing fabric approximately ¼" larger than the damage. Using a small spatula, push the backing fabric under the damaged area. For damaged areas smaller than ½", a backing is not necessary

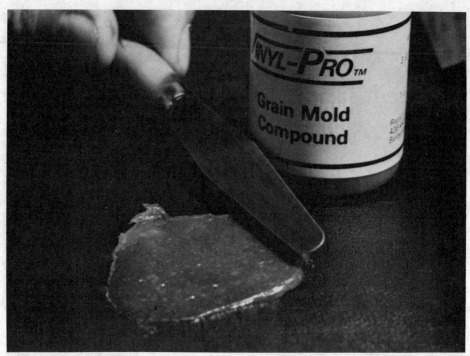

Step 3. Mix and match the color of your vinyl repair compound to the color of the vinyl being repaired

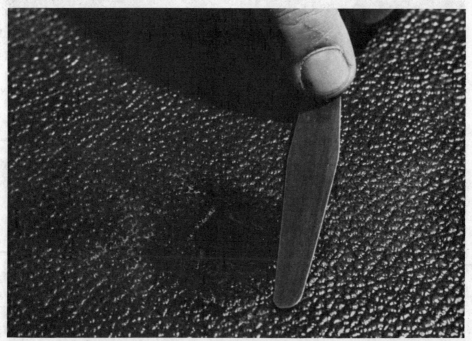

Step 4. Using a small spatula, fill in the damaged area evenly and remove any excess compound from the area. On deep grained vinyl tops, the center of the damaged area should be filled slightly higher than the edges. This will create a slight mound in the center of the repair, to allow it to accept the deep grain necessary

Step 5. Plug in the heat curing tool and allow it to warm for 3–5 minutes. Be careful—the entire tool except for the handle will get very hot. Hold the tool about ⅛" away from the repair compound and insert the plastic hose tip in your mouth. Select a piece of grain paper that matches the grain of your vinyl fabric and hold it with your other hand next to the area being repaired

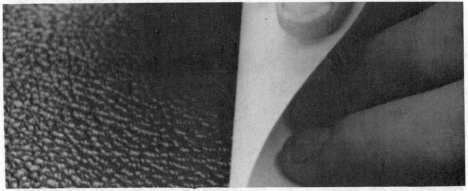

Step 6. Blow into the plastic tube and move the heat curing tool in a circular motion over the vinyl repair compound. The repair compound will get very hot and will probably smoke slightly. If the repair compound does not get hot enough (smoke slightly), it probably will not accept the grain from the grain paper. Instantly press the grain paper down on the hot repair compound and leave it there for a full minute. After it is cool, remove the grain paper and examine the repair. Any underfilled areas or small defects can be corrected by filling in the repair and repeating Step 5. Refill and regrain as often as necessary

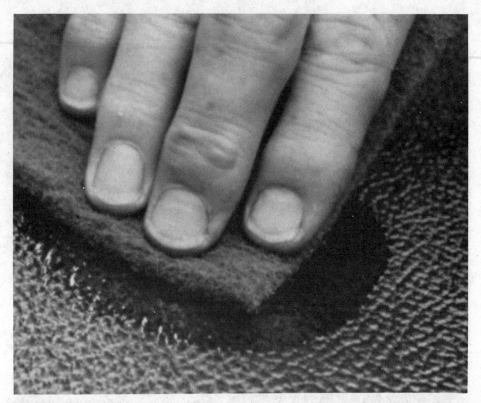

Step 7. Use a conventional vinyl top dressing to restore the shine over the repaired area

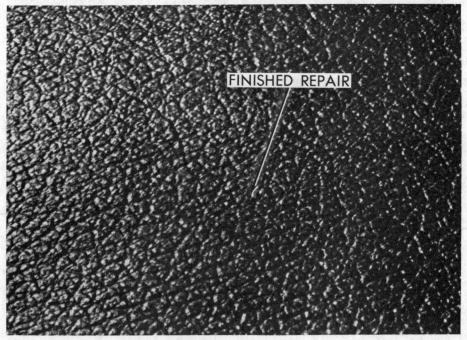

FINISHED REPAIR

Step 8. The repaired area is practically invisible

# 12

## REPAIR TWELVE

# Aligning Body Panels

Depending on the type of body repairs that are made and the location of the damage, it may be necessary to make some minor adjustments on doors, trunk lids or tailgates. The adjustments shown are typical examples of most cars.

You should also consult the chapter on repairing a Dented Trunk Lid or Hood for more information on straightening bent or misaligned hinges.

## DOORS AND HINGES

### Doors

If a door must be removed and reinstalled, or simply adjusted you should match-mark the position of the hinges on the door pillars. The holes of the hinges and/or the hinge attaching points are usually oversize to permit alignment of doors. The striker plate is also moveable, through oversize holes, permitting up-and-down, in-and-out and fore-and-aft movement. Fore-and-aft movement is made by adding or subtracting shims from behind the striker and pillar post. The striker should be adjusted so that the door closes fully and remains closed, yet enters the lock freely.

### Door Hinges

Don't try to cover up poor door adjustment with a striker plate adjustment. The gap on each side of the door should be equal and uniform and there should be no metal-to-metal contact as the door is opened or closed.

1. Determine which hinge bolts must be loosened to move the door in the desired direction.

2. Loosen the hinge bolt(s) just enough to allow the door to be moved with a padded pry bar.

3. Move the door a small amount and check the fit, after tightening the bolts. Be sure that there is no bind or interference with adjacent panels.

4. Repeat this until the door is properly positioned, and tighten all the bolts securely.

# HOOD, TRUNK OR TAILGATE

As with doors, the outline of hinges should be scribed before removal or adjustment. The hood and trunk can be aligned by loosening the hinge bolts in their slotted mounting holes and moving the hood or trunk lid as necessary. The hood and trunk have adjustable catch locations to regulate lock engagement bumpers at the front and/or rear of the hood provide a vertical adjustment and the hood lockpin can be adjusted for proper engagement.

The tailgate on the station wagon can be adjusted by loosening the hinge bolts in their slotted mounting holes and moving the tailgate on its hinges. The latchplate and latch striker at the bottom of the tailgate opening can be adjusted to stop rattle. An adjustable bumper is located on each side.

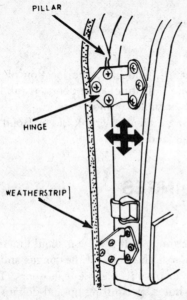

The door hinge holes, either where they bolt to the body or the door, are enlarged to permit adjustment horizontally and vertically

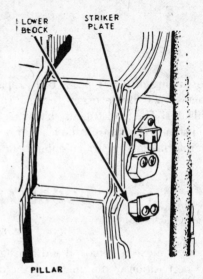

The door striker (attached to the body pillars) can be adjusted for proper lock engagement

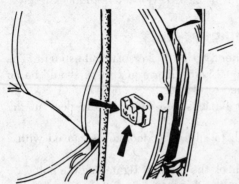

The striker plate and lower block are attached to the door and can also be adjusted for positive lock engagement

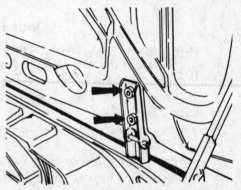

The hood or trunk hinge bolts (arrows) can be loosened to permit fore-and-aft adjustment

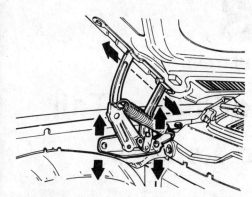

The height of the hood at the rear is adjusted by loosening the bolts that attach the hinge to the body and moving the hood up or down

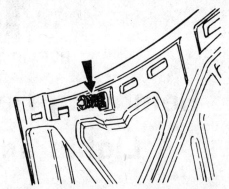

The end of the hood pin (arrow) is slotted and locked in place by a nut at the base of the pin. The pin can be turned in or out for proper lock engagement, after loosening the locknut

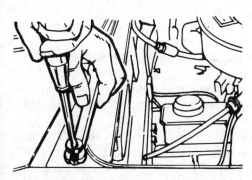

The height of the hood can also be adjusted with stop screws at the front and/or rear of the hood

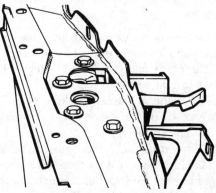

The base of the hood lock can also be repositioned slightly to give more positive lock engagement

# 13

**REPAIR THIRTEEN**

# Removing Headlights, Tail Lights and Lenses

In the course of making body repairs, it is often necessary to remove exterior lights and lenses in order to effect repairs or paint a panel.

There are many different exterior lighting arrangements, but basically only 2 ways to gain access to the lights.

Headlights are usually held in place by a retaining ring which may or may not be covered by part of the grille or nosepiece. The screws are almost always accessible from outside the car.

Turn signals, tail lights and parking lights are covered by a plastic lens. The lens retaining screws may be accessible from outside or they may have to be reached from behind the panel or through the trunk. In some cases, the entire housing may have to be removed from inside the trunk before the lens can be removed.

The following photos are typical examples of removal techniques.

# SINGLE HEADLIGHT

This single headlight on a Mustang II is typical of those held in place by a retaining ring covered by a trim piece.

Step 1. Remove the trim ring retaining screws. Don't disturb the headlight aiming screws located behind cut-outs in the trim ring (arrow). Remove the trim ring

Step 2. Remove the screws holding the retaining ring in place. Again, don't disturb the plastic headed headlight aiming screws

Step 3. Some retaining rings have one or two small rings that must be removed with pliers

Step 4. Remove the retaining ring

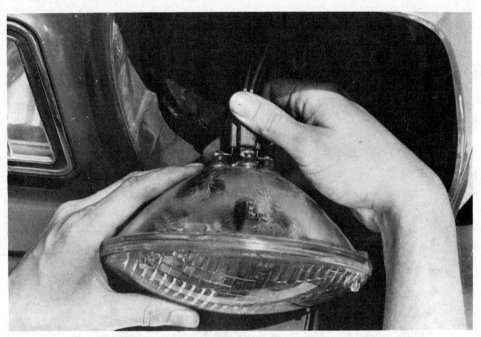

Step 5. Slide the headlight out of the housing (bucket) and remove the 3-pronged plug

Step 6. The headlight can be installed in the same manner as it was removed. A screwdriver can be used to hook the springs in position

# DUAL HEADLIGHTS

The duel headlights on this Chevrolet are typical of those that are accessible after removing a portion of the grille.

Step 1. The trim piece on this Chevy is part of the grille and must be removed for access to the headlight retaining ring. Don't disturb the headlight adjusting screws (arrows)

Step 2. Remove the screws holding the trim piece in place

Step 3. Remove the trim piece to expose the headlight retaining ring(s)

Step 4. Remove the 3 screws securing the headlight retaining ring. Don't disturb the plastic-headed headlight aiming screws (arrows)

Step 5.  Remove the headlight retaining ring and pull the headlight out of the bucket

Step 6.  Remove the 3-bladed plug from the back of the headlight

# SIDE MARKERS AND PARKING LIGHTS

Most parking lamp and side marker lenses can be removed from outside the car. In some cases, the retaining nuts are located behind the fender panel. These 2 examples are typical of common types.

The rear side marker lens on this Vega also serves as the bulb housing. Remove the 2 screws holding the lens/housing to the fender and unsnap the bulb socket from the lens

The front side marker lens on this Datsun was removed after removing 2 screws. If it is necessary to remove the lamp housing, it is held to the fender with sheet metal screws. Be sure you don't damage the gasket when removing the lens

# TAIL LIGHTS AND TURN SIGNAL LENSES

In most cases, the lens is removed from outside the car and the housing itself is removed from inside the trunk. In some cases, the entire housing can be removed from outside the car.

To remove the rear taillight lens from this Vega, remove 4 screws holding the chrome ring and lens in place. The housing is removed from inside the car

The entire rear taillight housing can be removed from this Plymouth Volare after removing 4 screws. Pull the lens and housing from the fender and unsnap the bulb holder from the housing

# 14

## REPAIRS FOURTEEN AND FIFTEEN

# Installing Body Side Molding

Next to rust and collision, crowded parking lots are your car's worst enemies. The dents and dings from careless shoppers opening their doors against your doors and fenders can be just as expensive as a minor accident. Body side moldings serve the dual purposes of dressing up the appearance of your car and protecting it from the hazards of parking lots.

## REPAIRS 14 AND 15

### Installing Body Side Moulding

**TIME REQUIRED:** ½–1½ hours

**TOOLS**

Grease pencil (china marker)
Tape measure or yardstick
Single edged razor blade
Electric drill ⎱
Rubber mallet ⎰
Shears        } Rivet-on
Rivet-gun       type only
Screwdriver ⎰

**MATERIALS**

Clean rag
Solvent (wax remover)
Masking tape
Rivets (rivet-on type only)
Body side molding kit

Body side molding kits are available in almost any well stocked parts store from a variety of manufacturers.

There are two basic types—self-adhering or rivet-on—available in 3 widths and in more than 30 colors to match almost any OEM color. Self-adhesive types typically come in rolls of narrow (approximately ½″ wide), medium (¾–1″) and wide (1-¼ to 1.¾″) widths, while rivet-on styles are normally available in 6-foot lengths of wide and narrow widths only.

Enough to do an average size car will cost from $10–15 and can be installed by anyone in about an hour, using commonly available hand tools. The only tool you might not have in your collection is a rivet gun (for rivet-on types) that can be rented or purchased inexpensively.

The last step is to carefully remove the masking tape, leaving you with a professional installation that will protect your car from parking lot dings and dents.

There are a few precautions that should be followed when performing any adhesive molding installation.

1. Let new paint age for at least 1 week before installing any adhesive molding.

2. Don't wash the car for at least 48 hours following the installation. This will allow the adhesive backing to "set" for a permanent job.

If for any reason, you should want to remove the molding, use a bug and tar remover to soften the adhesive and remove the molding. Any adhesive that remains can be removed with Formula 409, Prep-Sol or rubbing alcohol.

## INSTALLING ADHESIVE BODY SIDE MOLDING

Step 1. The car should be on a reasonably level surface and parked in the shade. Direct sunlight will make the adhesive backing too sticky and difficult to reposition. Use a steel tape and china marker to mark the position of the molding. It will generally be placed along the widest part of the car

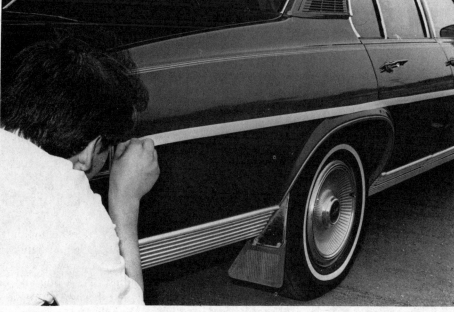

Step 2. Lay a strip of masking tape along the entire length of the car using the marks you've just made as a guide. Sight down the length of the tape to be sure it is straight. The top of the tape will act as a guide for the molding

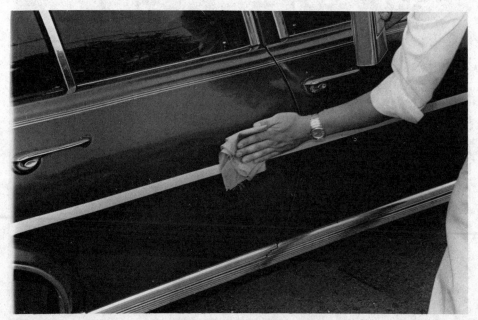

Step 3. Use a clean rag and a solvent to strip the wax from car where the molding will be applied. This is the most important step—you must get all the wax off. Prep-Sol® or household Formula 409 are good solvents, although rubbing alcohol will work with more rubbing effort

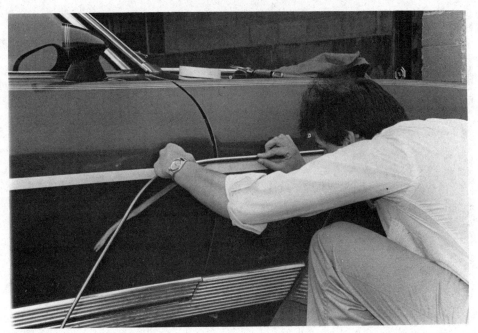

Step 4. Start at the front fender and peel off about 1' of backing at a time. Use the tape as a guide for the molding, and don't press too hard, so the molding can be repositioned if necessary

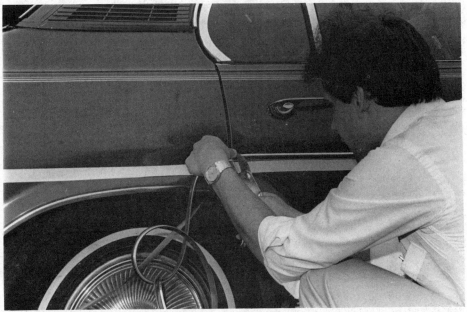

Step 5. When you get to the rear quarter panel, cut the molding in the center of the gap between the door and quarter panel. You can cut the molding with garden shears or a single edged razor blade

Step 6. Start the other spear end at the rear of the car and work towards the front, as you did in step 4

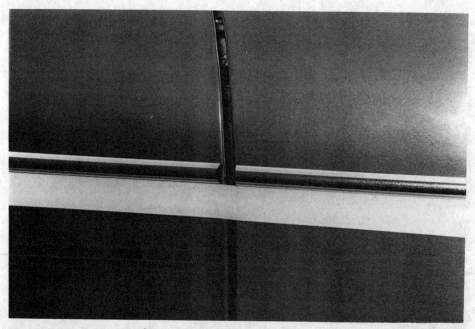

Step 7. Finish the installation by checking your work and trimming the molding ends. Use a razor blade to trim the molding at the trailing edge of the door square. The end of the molding on the leading edge of the door (arrow) should be trimmed at a 45° angle, so the molding will not "catch" when the door is opened. Go along the entire length of molding and bear down hard with the heel of your hand

## Installing Rivet-On Body Side Molding

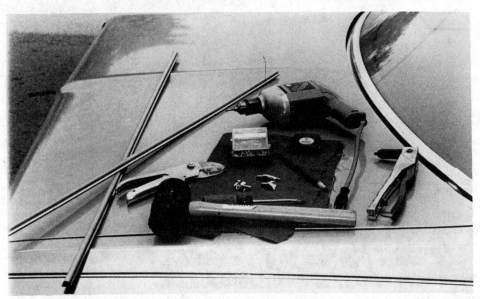

Step 1. To install rivet-on body side molding you'll need shears, screwdriver, rubber mallet, china marker, tape measure, 1/8" x 1/4" grip rivets and an electric drill with a 9/64" bit. It's easiest to use a drill bit 1/64" larger than the rivet shank

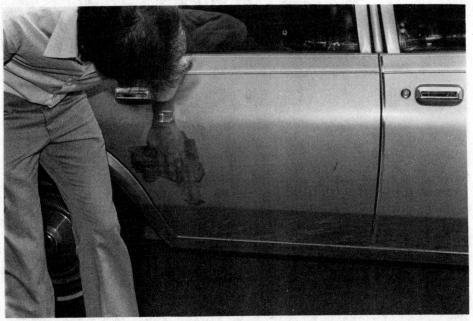

Step 2. Rivet-on molding can be installed on any temperature surface, but some molding manufacturers use a small adhesive strip to make installation easier. In these cases, it is advisable to wipe the car clean with a rag to allow the temporary adhesive to hold

Step 3. Mark the fenders and doors at the widest part of the car with a china marker

Step 4. Assemble a piece of molding and track, and mark the length required. Be sure to leave enough on each end (usually about ½″) for the caps and spears. Cut the molding to the size required. After cutting and measuring the first side, you can use these to make duplicate pieces for the other side

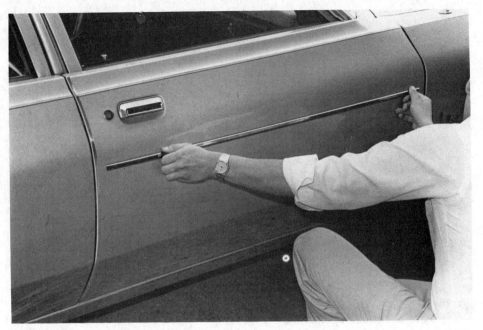

Step 5. Remove the molding from the track. If the track has an adhesive strip, peel off the backing and position the track according to the marks you made in step 3. If there is no adhesive strip, someone will have to hold the track in position. Be sure it is where you want it before drilling holes

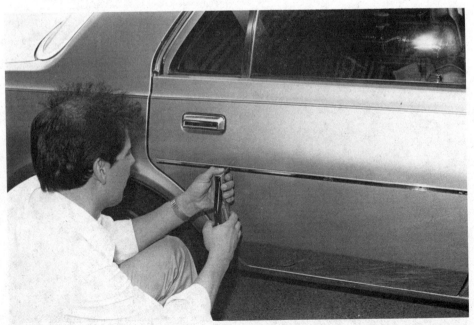

Step 6. Using the holes in the track as a guide, drill each hole and an additional hole ¾" from each end. Using a rivet gun, install the rivets. Be sure to squeeze the rivet tightly

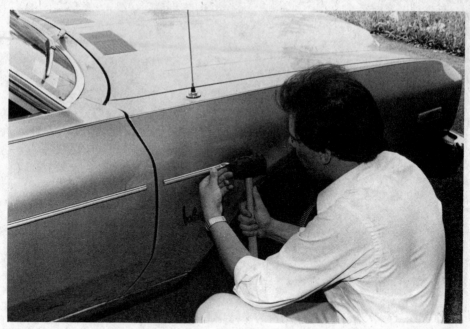

Step 7.  Install the plastic molding in the track and finish the job by installing the end caps and spears. It may be necessary to tap the caps and spears into the track with a mallet

Step 8.  The finished job gives a neat, original equipment look that will last the life of the car

# 15

# Preparing Your Car for a New Paint Job

Unless you have, or have access to, the necessary equipment, you would be wise to leave painting an entire car to professionals. You'll get a far better job, and it won't cost much more than it would for you to rent or buy the equipment and purchase the materials. Your largest saving will result from preparing the car for painting. If you get the car ready to paint at home, you can (1) get a perfect job because you can take all the time you need to get it right, and (2) save yourself about two-thirds of the cost of a new paint job. What most people don't know is that most of the high cost of completely refinishing an automobile is the labor of preparing it for spraying. The actual time it takes to spray a car is only about one-half hour. So . . . if your car is destined for a bright, new, shiny finish, roll up your sleeves and let's get started. If you follow the simple procedures and take your time to do it right, you can stand back and look at a beautiful finished product. If you really want to paint the car yourself, see the Chapter on Painting Techniques.

There are four basic steps to follow when completely refinishing an auto.

1. Pre-clean the complete body from bumper to bumper with a good pre-cleaning solvent.

2. Feather-edge all nicks, scratches and slight imperfections in the old finish. If you have done any body work using this book as a guide, then all of the old finish edges that were ground back must be feather-edged at this time. Spot prime all these areas and block sand them with a paint paddle and 220-grit open face sandpaper.

3. Sand the complete car with 320-grit open face sandpaper.

4. Using masking tape and newspaper, tape off all areas that are not to be painted such as bumpers, moldings, glass, etc.

The following instructions for preparing your car for refinishing include many professional techniques so that the finished product will be nothing short of perfect. There is only one way to do a job, and that way is, of course, the right way. Otherwise the material you purchase and the time and energy you spend will be wasted.

# LIST OF MATERIALS

This list of supplies includes everything you will need to prepare your car for refinishing. They can be purchased at any auto supply or auto paint supply store, and most large discount stores. When you buy these supplies, do not purchase the paint. The paint is supplied by the shop that is going to apply the finish. The reason for this is that different painters use different brands. They are used to their favorite brand and do their best work with it, so let them buy the paint. You will need:

One gallon of pre-cleaning solvent.

Two or three wooden paint paddles.

Three rolls of ¾-in. masking tape.

Twelve sheets of 220-grit open face sandpaper.

Twelve sheets of 320-grit open face sandpaper.

One or two spray cans of lacquer base primer.

Don't over-buy on these items, as you can always go back for more if you run out.

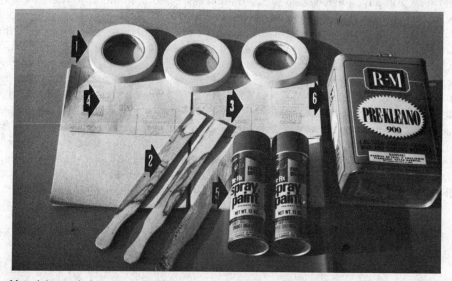

Materials needed to prepare your car for a new paint job

# STEP 1—PRE-CLEANING THE BODY

The very first step in preparing the car for refinishing is to remove all foreign substances from the old finish, including wax, road tars, tree sap, etc. They must be completely removed to insure that the new paint film will completely adhere to the old finish.

For this job you need a good pre-cleaning solvent. Before you use the solvent, read the label and do exactly as it says with no short cuts. This is a very important step if you expect your new finish to last. Do one panel at a time, such as a complete fender, so as not to miss a spot accidentally that could give trouble later.

This high contrast photo shows the wet area when using the precleaner. Do about 12 square inches at a time. Apply the cleaner, and while the area is still wet, wipe dry

Most pre-cleaner labels will tell you to wipe an area with solvent on a clean rag and, while the surface is still wet, wipe it dry with a clean rag. The rag dampened with the solvent loosens the foreign substance and the clean dry rag wipes it from the old finish. This leaves it clean and ready for the following operations. Change rags often. When you are certain you have done this first step completely, move on to Step 2.

## STEP 2—FEATHER-EDGING AND SPOT PRIMING- BLOCK SANDING

The second step is feather-edging the old finish wherever it is broken or interrupted; for example, a stone bruise or a nick where someone has opened a car door into the side of your car, etc. You must also feather-edge any areas where you have done any body work and have ground the old finish back to make room for your metal finishing. The reason for this is very obvious if you think about it for a moment. First of all, think of the old finish as having some degree of thickness. A coat of paint is only a film covering the metal, but it does, in fact, have thickness. Any interruptions, such as scratches or chips, will cause a hole in the film. If you were to cover this hole in the old finish with a coat of bright shiny paint, it would be highlighted.

What you have to do is build the hole or low area back up to the level of the old finish with primer. Sand the area of the hole to taper the abrupt edge of the hole gradually out to the level of the old finish. When this is done, simply spot prime a couple of times and, when dry, block sand with 220-grit sandpaper and a paint paddle. Feel the area with the flat of your hand. If it is perfectly smooth, go on to the next area. If you still feel a slight low spot, prime it again and block it down when dry.

The illustrations show such nicks and scratches and just how they are treated.

A. Feather-edge the hole or scratch in the old finish with 220-grit paper and paddle so that it gradually tapers out to the level of the old finish.

B. Spot spray with lacquer-type primer, two or three coats, allowing each coat to dry before applying the next one.

C. Block sand with the 220-grit paper and paddle when the primer is dry.

I've talked about doing a job and doing it well, without taking any shortcuts. Well, here is a short cut to certain failure, one I have seen many times, both in professional shops and on do-it-yourself jobs. Instead of going through the sand and prime operation step-by-step, glazing putty is wiped into these small imperfections and when dry, leveled off with the old finish. This sounds easy, but that glob of filler that is wiped into the hole in the old finish is destined to become a *pop-out*. It will do just that, pop-out and take the paint that is covering it along.

The reason this method doesn't work is very simple. When you feather-edge the damage in the old finish, tapering the abrupt edge gradually out to the level of the old finish, and apply primer, it becomes a part of the film covering the metal. When one stuffs a gob of putty in the hole, it is not a part of the film, as it has definite edges. It becomes only a sort of plug or insert in the old finish. When the new paint is applied, with all it's "chemical hotness," the putty or filler becomes soft and sooner or later is dislodged. This, of course, leaves you with the same hole.

A similar process is used for a large area such as one that you have repaired. The edge of the old finish has to be gradually feather-edged and the metal finished area has to be built up with primer and then the entire area block sanded with a paint paddle and 220-grit sandpaper. Once these damaged areas in the old finish are taken care of, you are ready to go on to Step 3. Be certain to do a good job on Step 2. This is where most do-it-yourselfers fail.

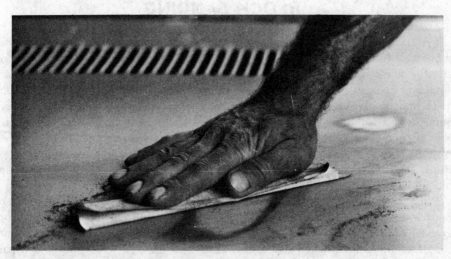

Feather-edging a typical nick or hole in the old finish with 220-grit and paint paddle

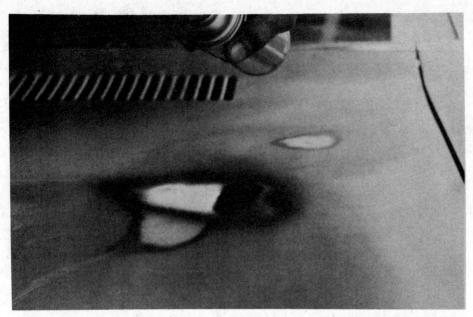

Priming the area just feather-edged to bring the void up to the level of the old finish

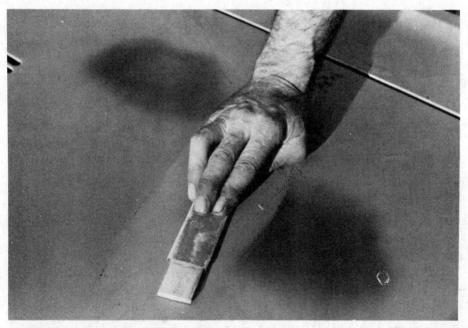

Block sanding with the same 220-grit paper and paddle. If the void can still be felt, repeat the operation

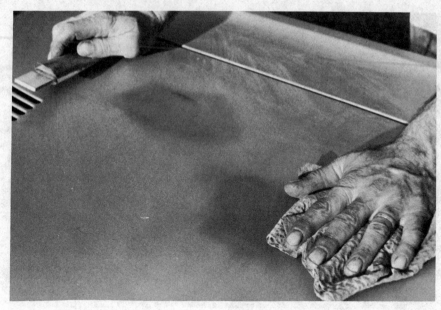

When properly done, the finish should be smooth and look like this

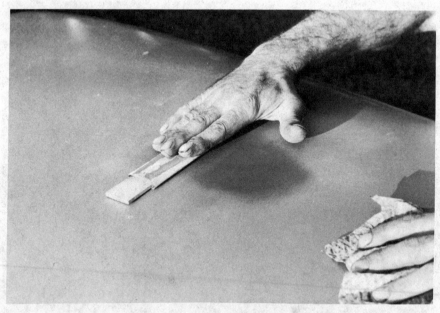

The same treatment is given to all holes, nicks and scratches in the old finish. Feather-edge the bad spot, prime, and block sand to make the area level with the old finish

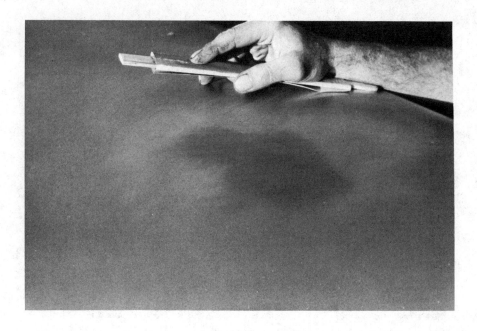

A good example of scratches in the old finish

Feather-edge the scratches with 220-grit and paddle

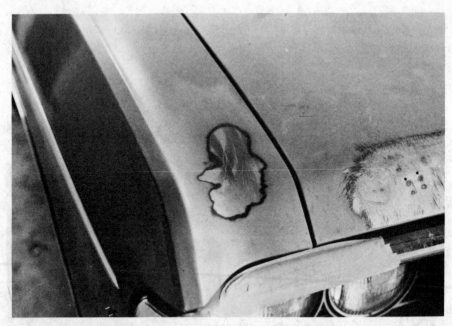

Properly feather-edged, the scratched area should look like this

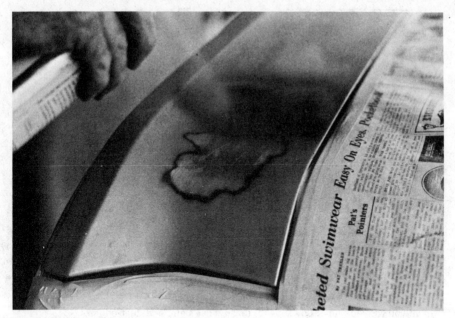

Temporarily mask off the area and prime it

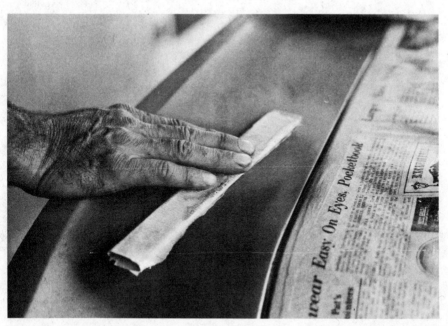

After primer is dry, block sand the area. If you can still feel the void, repeat the operation

If you've made any body repairs, these must also be feather-edged

Repaired areas should look like this before priming

Prime all metal finished areas after featheredging. When primer has dried, block sand with 220-grit and paddle. If the area is still not smooth, reprime and block sand again. Keep repeating this operation until the area is smooth and you can feel no imperfections with the palm of your hand

The area is primed again, since portions of metal and filler show through. It will be sanded again when you sand the complete car

# STEP 3—SANDING THE COMPLETE CAR

Step 3, sanding the complete car, is another project that should be done panel-by-panel. Do one panel completely before going on to the next. This step is the next-to-most-tedious part of preparing to refinish, but it is, in fact, just about the most important. The better you do this step, the better the finish you're going to end up with, and most important, the longer it will hold up.

Take a sheet of 320-grit open face sandpaper and fold it in half from the top to the bottom. Crease it, and tear the paper in half. Take one of the halves and fold it in

You're now ready to sand the complete car with 320-grit paper and lots of patience

Tear the sandpaper in half, and then fold each half in thirds

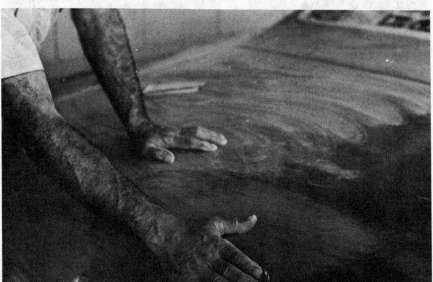

Sand in straight lines back and forth in an area about twelve inches square. Sand until the old finish is completely smooth and full. Sand over all the areas that were primed as well. Be sure all the scratches and imperfections are sanded out on these areas

thirds. This gives you a good sized piece for palming. Start sanding on any panel, sanding in straight lines back and forth. As the paper tends to build up with sanding dust, knock it against your free hand to reduce clogging. Sand an area about twelve inches square until the old finish is completely dull and you feel no imperfections as you run your hand over your work. The reason for sanding until the old finish is completely dull is to insure complete bonding of the new finish. Of course, you are feeling with your free hand to detect any small nicks or foreign matter that might be in the old finish.

Continue until the entire car is sanded. Care must be taken to sand every square inch of your car's sheet metal, right up to the very edge of moldings, door handles, hood emblems, etc. If you are having trouble sanding close to the edge of these items without scratching them, tape them over temporarily to protect them. If rust appears to be creeping out from under any of these trim pieces, it may be best to remove them. When you have them off, you can sand the finish down to bare metal and prime as in the feather-edging process. Otherwise, do not remove these items and disturb their factory installation. Getting in close to items like windshield wiper shafts where they go through the cowl, door handles, door locks, etc. is very time consuming, but very necessary to prevent your new paint job from peeling in just a few months, so do it. Sand the entire surface no matter how hard it is to get at, if you want a top-flight professional job. On the feather-edged areas and the areas that

When sanding the complete car, be careful to sand right up to the very edge of moldings and door handles. If you don't, the paint will soon peel from these areas

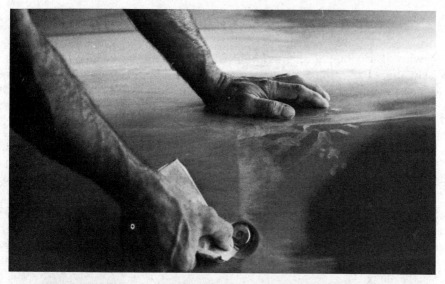

Here are two areas that are hard to get at, but they must be sanded if you want a good paint job

you repaired, continue to sand just as you are sanding the rest of the car. Look closely at these areas for grinder marks and coarse sandpaper scratches.

If you sand through to bare metal, reprime that area and work around that spot until it dries. Then go back and sand it again. Usually, you won't be able to feel these marks in the primer. You have to look closely for them, and they must be sanded out. If they are not taken care of they will show in the finished product.

When you have sanded the whole car, just to be sure of your work, go back and check the areas that were feather-edged and primed and any areas that were repaired. These are trouble spots that can ruin an otherwise good job. When you have doublechecked your work and are satisfied with it, you have completed Step 3.

# STEP 4—MASKING THE CAR

This is a fairly simple operation but is probably the most tedious. If it is done quickly, items like chrome moldings, emblems, window glass will get paint on them and look thoroughly shabby when the job is finished. A poorly masked car is the result of amateur work. There is no set rule for masking, as we all do it differently. The end result is the important factor.

1. All items that are not to receive paint must be completely masked with tape and/or paper. This includes windows, bumpers, and vinyl tops. Be as neat as possible. Avoid pockets in the paper where dust can gather and cause a dirty finished product.

2. For safety's sake, no windows or lights of any kind should be masked until the car is driven to the shop that will do the painting. If the car is to be driven some distance to the shop, don't paper the grille or the car may overheat. Don't expect the painter to do it though or the price will go up! Do it yourself when you have the car at the shop.

3. Do not mask until a day or two before taking the car to the shop. The longer masking tape stays on the car the harder it will be to get off. Don't let the car get wet once you start masking. Water can get trapped and then blown out on the finish as the painter is applying the paint.

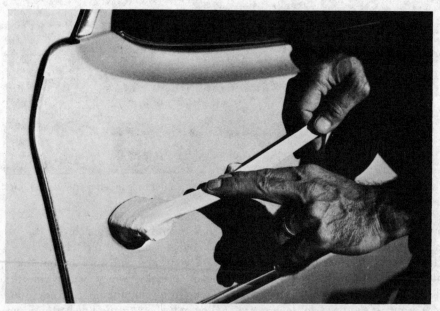

Taping a door handle. It is better to leave a small part of the handle exposed than to get too close to the body and possibly pull the fresh paint off when you untape the car

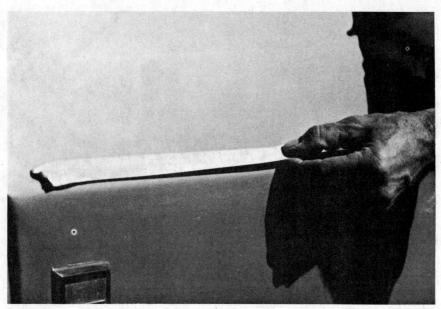

Tape moldings in the same manner as door handles. Be sure that the tape doesn't touch the body

A typical masked section. Notice that all taping is neatly done

The pen reminds you not to get any tape on any part of the sheet metal to be painted. Naturally, when you untape the car that portion under the tape wouldn't have any paint on it

Taping is a time-consuming job, but it must be done. Some emblems can be removed and some can't. Take your time and do it right

# CAUSES AND PREVENTION
# OF PAINTING AND REFINISHING PROBLEMS

It is helpful for the do-it-yourself painter to understand why certain conditions occur in the finished job. This understanding, coupled with effective painting techniques, is essential to the best results. This section shows a number of common conditions that can occur and their probable causes and remedies.

## Bleeding

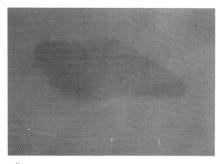

Bleeding

**APPEARANCE**
Discoloration of the surface of refinish color.
**CAUSE**
Solvent penetration from fresh color material dissolves old finish, usually reds and maroons, releasing a dye that comes to the surface.
**REMEDY**
1. Remove all color coats and recoat, or
2. Allow surface to cure, then apply bleeder sealer and recoat.
**PREVENTION**
Apply bleeder sealer over suspected bleeder colors before spraying new color.

## Crazing, Cracking or Checking

Crazing

**APPEARANCE**
Surface formulation like shattered glass.

Cracking or checking

**APPEARANCE**
Crowfoot separation (check).
Irregular separation (cracking).
**CAUSES**
1. Insufficient drying of films prior to recoating.
2. Repeated extreme temperature changes.
3. Excessive heavy coats (cold checking).
4. Paint ingredients not thoroughly mixed.
5. Adding materials to a product not designed for it (incompatibility).
6. Recoating a previously checked finish.
7. Thinner attacking the strained surface of a cured acrylic lacquer (crazing).
**REMEDY**
Remove finish down through checked paint film and refinish.
**PREVENTION**
1. Follow proper drying times between coats.
2. Avoid extreme temperature changes.
3. Spray uniform coats, avoiding excess particularly with lacquers.
4. Mix all ingredients thoroughly.
5. Use only recommended materials (thinners, etc.)
6. Remove a previously checked finish before recoating.

## Blistering

**APPEARANCE**
1. Small swelled areas like a water blister on human skin.
2. Lack of gloss if blisters are minute.
3. Broken edged craters if the blisters have burst.

Blistering

## CAUSES
1. Rust under surface.
2. Painting over oil or grease.
3. Moisture in spray lines.
4. Prolonged or repeated exposure of film to high humidity.

## REMEDY
Sand and refinish blistered areas.

## PREVENTIONS
1. Thoroughly clean and treat metal.
2. Frequently drain air line of water.
3. Avoid use of overly fast thinners when temperature is high.
4. Allow proper dry times between coatings.

## Fisheyes

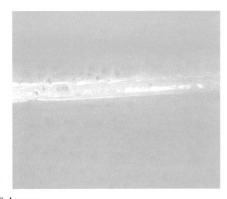

Fisheyes

## APPEARANCE
Previous finish can be seen in spots.

## CAUSES
1. Improper cleaning of old surface.
2. Spraying over finishes that contain silicone.

## REMEDY
Wash off paint while still wet.

## PREVENTION
1. Clean surface with wax and grease remover.
2. Use fisheye preventer in finish coats to be sprayed over old films containing silicone.

## Rust Under The Finish

### APPEARANCE
1. Peeling or blistering.
2. Raised surface spots.

Rust under the finish

### CAUSES
1. Improper metal preparation.
2. Broken paint film allows moisture to creep under surrounding finish.

### REMEDY
1. Seal off entrance of moisture from inner parts of panels.
2. Sand down to bare metal, prepare metal and treat with rust remover/inhibitor before painting.

### PREVENTION
1. Locate source of moisture and seal off.
2. When replacing ornaments or molding, be careful not to break paint film and allow dissimilar metals to come in contact. This contact can produce electrolysis that may cause a tearing away or loss of good bond with the film.

## Runs

### APPEARANCE
1. Running of wet paint film in rivulets.
2. Mass slippage of total film.

### CAUSES
1. Over reduction with low air pressure.
2. Extra slow thinners.
3. Painting on cold surface.
4. Improperly cleaned surface.

### REMEDY
Wash off and refinish.

## PREVENTION

1. Use recommended thinner at specified reduction and air pressure.
2. Do not paint over cold surface.
3. Clean surface thoroughly.

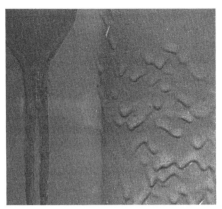

Runs and sags

## APPEARANCE

Partial slipping of paint in the form of curtains.

## CAUSES

1. Under reduction.
2. Applying successive coats without allowing dry time between coats.
3. Low air pressue (lack of atomization).
4. Gun too close.
5. Gun out of adjustment.

## REMEDY

Sand or wash off and refinish.

## PREVENTION

1. Use proper thinner at recommended reduction.
2. Adjust air pressure and gun for correct atomization.
3. Keep gun at right distance from work.

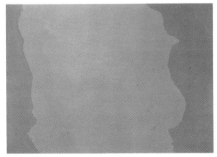

Plastic bleed-through

## APPEARANCE

Discoloration (normally yellowing) of the top coat color.

## CAUSES

1. Too much hardener.
2. Applying top coat before plastic is cured.

## REMEDY

1. Remove patch, or
2. Cure top coat, sand and refinish.

## PREVENTION

1. Use correct amount of hardener.
2. Allow adequate cure time before refinishing.

Orange peel

## APPEARANCE

Resembles the skin of an orange.

## CAUSES

1. Under reduction.
2. Improper thinning solvent.
3. Improper flow.
4. Surface drying too fast.
5. Improper air pressure.

## REMEDY

1. (Enamel) Rub surface with a mild polishing compound. (Lacquer) Sand or use rubbing compound.
2. Sand and refinish.

## PREVENTION

1. Proper air and gun adjustment.
2. Proper thinning solvents.

## APPEARANCE

Small craters or appearance like over spray.

## CAUSE

Same as Blistering (except blisters have broken).

**REMEDY**
See "Blistering"
**PREVENTION**
See "Blistering"

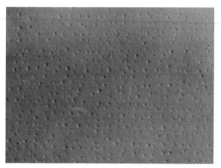
Pitting or cratering

## Water Spotting

**APPEARANCE**
1. Dulling of gloss in spots.

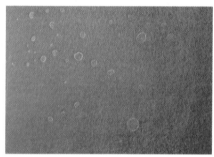
Water spotting

2. Mass of spots that appear as a large distortion of the film.

**CAUSES**
1. Spots of water drying on finish that is not thoroughly dry.
2. Washing finish in bright sunlight.

**REMEDY**
Sand and refinish.

**PREVENTION**
1. Keep fresh paint job out of rain.
2. Do not allow water to dry on new finish.

## Wet Spots

**APPEARANCE**
Discolored or slow drying spots of various sizes.

**CAUSES**
1. Improper cleaning.
2. Excessively heavy undercoats not properly dried.
3. Sanding with gasoline or other chemically contaminated solvent.

**REMEDY**
Sand or wash off thoroughly and refinish.

**PREVENTION**
1. Clean surface with wax and grease remover.
2. Allow undercoats to dry thoroughly.
3. Use only water as a sanding lubricant.

*Photographs courtesy PPG Industries, Ditzler Automotive Finishes, Southfield, Michigan*

When taping an antenna, don't spiral the tape, instead, tape the length of the unit. It will be much easier to remove the tape

When taping the windows, be very neat and avoid pockets and folds in the paper that can trap dirt and cause a dirty final product. CAUTION: Do not tape windows or lights until the car is at the paint shop

# STEP 5—GETTING THE CAR PAINTED

By now you should be just about ready for paint. If you are going to paint the car yourself, see the chapter on Painting Techniques. If you are going to have someone else paint the car, and haven't already lined up someone to do the job, call around to do your pricing rather than taking the car to different shops. Like everything else, price is not the only consideration. After all the work you've put in, quality is equally important. Your best bet is to look in the Yellow Pages of your phone book and jot down two or three addresses of independent body shops. Don't bother going to any of the new car dealers, as they are always loaded with work, and probably wouldn't do your job.

Talk to your friends or people at a local body shop. Frequently there is someone locally who works as a painter in a shop and "moonlights" out of his own garage at nights. You can get very satisfactory results this way, but the job is almost always a cash deal. Don't forget to contact the local franchised paint shops, as most do quality work at reasonable prices. Frequently you'll find that many body shops send their work to these painters, rather than paint an entire car themselves.

When you talk to the man at the shop, say, "I have prepared my car for painting and would like to know how much you charge for applying a sealer coat and spraying the paint."

Be sure they are planning to seal your old finish before they paint, as sealing is important for good adhesion, good gloss, and good coverage of any minor imperfections you may have missed.

One thing to remember when you ask about getting your paint work done: The people you are dealing with are professionals. They are always busy and are trying to make money. Use the humble approach, and don't try to make them think you are an old hand at their game. They'll find you out before you have said ten words. Simply tell them you have prepped your car and you would like them to refinish it. If they brush you off, thank them for their time and go to another shop. It will mean they have more work than they can handle. When you find a shop that will look at your car or panel, they will see you have done a good job and will give you a price.

# CARE AND MAINTENANCE OF A NEW FINISH

After your car is repainted, put back any items you removed prior to painting such as moldings or emblems. For the next thirty days be very careful of the new finish, as it will be soft and quite vulnerable to nicks and scratches. Keep the car out of the hot sun as much as possible, and keep the finish free of dirt. To wash the car for the first two weeks, just rinse it off with clear water from a garden hose and wipe it dry with a clean, soft cloth. After two weeks you may wash the car with clean, soft rags and a mild soap solution. Be sure the soap is mild! Do not use harsh detergents!

Do not wax the car for at least thirty days, as the new finish has to breathe in order to dry properly. Before you wax the car, see the chapter on body care.

# 16

# Painting Techniques

Painting an automobile or an entire panel is a skill gained from years of experience. There is far more to painting then simply squeezing the trigger on the paint gun and hoping for the best.

Once you have completed the body repairs and primed the repair area you're ready to think about the finish coat of paint, and whether you are going to "shoot" the paint yourself or have it done professionally. There are several factors to consider:

There are basically 3 kinds of repair where paint is concerned—spot finishing, panel finishing and complete repaint jobs. The vast majority of minor auto body work falls into the spot refinishing category, which is easily handled by an aerosol spray can. These are inexpensive, easy to use and will produce quality finishes.

Repainting an entire panel is usually necessary after fairly extensive body work or in cases where a spot repair will be difficult to match the exact color. This is frequently the case with silver cars or those with metallic paint finishes. An entire panel is usually painted with a commercial spray gun and compressor, which can be rented, borrowed, or is available to purchase in do-it-yourself models from manufacturers of power equipment.

Repainting an entire car should be done with a spray gun and compressor.

## EQUIPMENT

Of primary importance is a clean, dry place to work. Dirt and dust have an affinity for wet paint and nothing will give your fresh paint job a worse looking surface than dirt and dust that settle in the paint.

For larger repairs, a compressor and spray gun can be purchased, rented or borrowed. The most common types of spray equipment are the syphon cup spray gun, in which trigger action controls both air and paint flow and the electric compressor with a storage tank reservoir. This equipment is frequently designed for automotive use and will produce excellent results when used properly.

# REFINISHING SYSTEMS

The refinishing system is basically the type of paint being used. The choice will be made from one of the 4 basic systems below.

## Acrylic Lacquer

Acrylic lacquer is relatively easy to apply and dries quickly. It provides excellent color and gloss, but does require more application time, as it must be applied in several color coats. Its cost is also slightly more and it must be buffed and compounded to bring up the high gloss.

## Synthetic Enamel

Synthetic enamels require fewer top coats, do not need compounding or buffing and cost less than other enamels. They dry to a high gloss, but require more drying time.

## Acrylic Enamel

Acyrilic enamels combine the best features of the Synthetic enamel and acrylic lacquer. They are easy to apply, dry quickly and no compounding or buffing is necessary. Acrylic enamel dries to a hard, durable finish but should be recoated with sealer after about 6 hours. Coat is between acrylic lacquer and synthetic enamel.

## Urethane Enamel

Urethane enamel is one of the newest, most sophisticated automotive finishes. It is expensive, but gives all the advantages of acrylic enamel, but is highly resistant to chemicals, nicks and scratches.

# BEFORE YOU BEGIN TO PAINT

There are several important preparatory steps you must take prior to actually painting that will go a long way toward assuring a satisfactory job.

The paint code is usually located on a metal tag affixed to the radiator support, door pillar or similar place. Check the paint code to be sure of the exact color

## Check the Paint Type & Color

The paint code is usually listed on a special tag affixed to the car either under the hood or on the door post. This code is the exact color for the original equipment paint on the vehicle. The code should be used when purchasing paint unless you plan to change the color. The reason for this is that some types of paint are incompatible without the use of special sealers.

Acrylic lacquer, for instance, can be used over old lacquer and acrylic lacquer with little surface preparation, assuming that the old finish is not rusted, severely checked, or otherwise deficient. Acrylic lacquer can also be used over enamel, but first it is generally recommended that the enamel be sanded thoroughly and sprayed with a sealer to assure good adhesion and minimize sand scratches marring the finish.

If you aren't sure which type of old painted surface you are working with, moisten a cloth with lacquer thinner and rub the finish. If it dissolves easily with little or no rubbing, it is lacquer; if it dissolves easily with considerable rubbing, it is acrylic lacquer; if it doesn't budge even with brisk rubbing, it is enamel.

Armed with the paint code and type of paint, you can purchase aerosol spray cans from a rack or you can purchase paint in bulk from your automotive paint supplier.

Do-it-yourself paints for small repairs are sold in spray cans or small bottles for touch-up work

Check the application book from the paint supplier for the exact color and code that you need

# SURFACE PREPARATION

## Aerosol Spray Can (Small Areas)

Once the repair is made and the area primed you are ready to paint. Just be sure the surrounding paint is clean and dry, and all wax is removed.

## Spray Gun (Larger Areas)

1. Remove the old finish—Several methods can be used. Among them are power sanding, hand sanding or specially formulated liquid paint removers. On fiberglass surfaces, it is safer to sand the paint, rather than use paint remover.

2. Metal Preparation—This is the most important step for good paint adhesion. Remove all traces of corrosion from the surface, by sanding. Wash the surface with a wax or grease remover and follow this with a metal conditioner and rust inhibitor to remove invisible rust. Wipe the entire panel with a tack rag to remove dust and dirt. Coat the bare metal with primer or primer surfaces.

3. Fiberglass Preparation—Fiberglass should be treated the same as metal, except that it is not corrosive and does not require treatment for rust. Thoroughly clean the surface with wax and grease remover.

Sand exposed fiberglass with 220 grit paper by hand and wipe the surface dry with clean rags. Wipe the entire surface with a tack rag, and prime the exposed surfaces.

4. Preparation of Old Paint—Wash the entire surface with wax and grease remover. Sand out any defects in the old finish and feather-edge all edges. Reclean the surface and treat the metal areas as above. Prime or seal the old paint as follows:

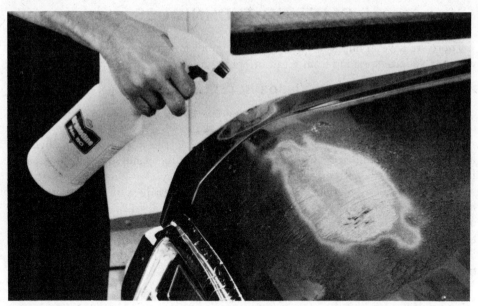

Wax and grease remover should be followed with a metal conditioner to remove invisible rust

If the old surface is enamel use an all-purpose primer-surface followed by acrylic enamel or acrylic lacquer.

If the old finish is lacquer, prime the surface with all-purpose primer-surfacer followed by enamel or lacquer.

If the old finish is acrylic, prime the surface with all purpose primer-surfacer followed by acrylic lacquer or acrylic enamel.

A primer-surfacer should be used to prime and seal the old paint. Finish the primer-surfacer by wet sanding with 400 paper

# PAINTING TECHNIQUES

There are several important things to remember for a good paint job regardless of whether you are spraying from a can or spray gun.

## Spraying Viscosity (Spray Gun Only)

The material should be thinned to spraying viscosity according to the directions on the can. Use the recommended thinner or reducer.

Measurement of the thinner is the only way to do the job adequately. Because appearance is affected by the temperature, the way the paint runs off the stirring paddle is not a reliable method of determining viscosity.

The amount of reduction should be the same regardless of temperature. At higher temperatures the viscosity of the reduced material will be lower but this is offset by a faster evaporation rate of the thinner as it travels between the gun and the surface. The result is that the paint reaches the surface at the correct viscosity.

The reverse is true in a cold shop. Reduced paint is a little thicker, but evaporation in the air is less so that the paint reaches the surface at the proper viscosity.

## Temperature

The temperature at which paint is sprayed and dries has great influence on the overall quality. This involves not only the surrounding air temperatures but the temperature of the surface as well. The surface should be approximately the same temperature as the surrounding air temperature. Spraying warm paint on a cold surface or spraying cool paint on a hot surface will completely upset the paint characteristics. The rate of evaporation on a hot summer day is approximately 50% faster than it is on an average day with an air temperature of 72°. Appropriate thinners or reducers should be used for warm and cold weather applications, as recommended by the manufacturer.

## Film Thickness

In general, the thicker the film applied, the longer the drying time.

The difference in film thickness will show up plainly in enamel colors. A lacquer that can be sanded in 30 minutes will take over an hour if sprayed twice as thick.

The reason is that the thicker the film the greater the depth of paint from which the thinner or reducer must work its way out, and, in enamels, the greater the distance the oxygen from the air must penetrate.

You should develop a technique so that the paint will remain wet long enough for proper flow-out, and no longer. Heavier coats are not necessary, and they may produce sags, curtains or wrinkles.

The amount of material sprayed on a surface with one stroke of the gun will depend on width of fan, distance from gun, air pressure at the gun, reduction, speed of stroke, and selection of thinner or reducer.

## Distance

Spray guns are designed to give the best performance at a distance of 8–12″ from the surface. If the spraying is done from a shorter distance, the high velocity of the spraying air tends to ripple the wet film. If the distance is increased beyond that there will be a greater percent of thinner evaporated, resulting in orange peel or dry film and, adversely effect color where matching is required. A slower evaporating thinner will permit more variation in the distance of the spray gun from the job, it will produce runs, if the gun gets too close. Excessive spraying distance also causes a loss in materials due to overspray.

### Strokes and Overlapping

If the gun is tilted toward the surface so that the fan pattern is not uniform, or if the gun is swung in an arc, varying the distance from the nozzle to the work, the paint will go on wetter where the nozzle is closer to the surface and drier where it is farther away. The gun should be at right angles to the job at all times. Do not fan the gun and do not use wrist motions if you want a uniform film. The only time it is permissible to fan the gun is on a small spot spray where the paint film at the edges of the spot should be thinner than the center portion. Work to a wet edge by using a fifty percent overlap and direct the center of the spray fan at the lower or nearest edge of the previous stroke.

## PAINTING WITH AEROSOL SPRAY CANS

1. Before painting, shake the can for almost 1 minute to thoroughly mix the paint. The paint is mixed when you can no longer hear the agitator ball inside the can.

2. Hold the can 8–12 inches from the work.

3. Spray with smooth strokes, keeping the can the same direction from the work and perpendicular to it.

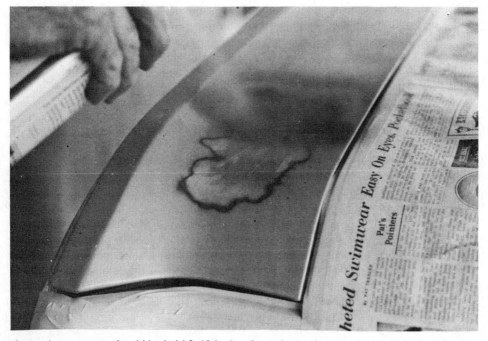

Aerosol spray cans should be held 8–12 inches from the work

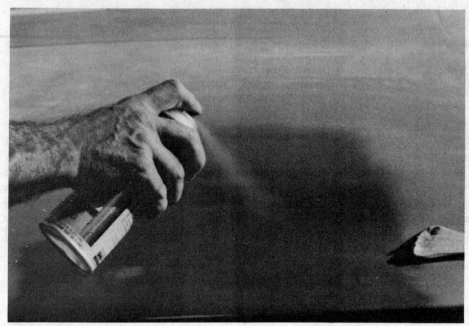

Keep the can perpendicular to the work and spray with long even strokes. Apply several thin coats about 30 seconds apart

4. Apply several thin coats, about 30 seconds apart. The final coat should appear glossy.

5. Let the paint dry thoroughly and inspect the surface. Runs or an orange peel surface can be sanded out, reprimed and repainted. If the surface is uniformly glossy and to your satisfaction, no further painting is necessary.

6. Allow the final coat to dry thoroughly. Don't be in too big a hurry to remove the masking tape, as this only produces paint ridges and lines.

7. You are now ready to blend the new paint job with the surrounding area.

## PAINTING WITH A SPRAY GUN

1. Mix the paint and thinner accurately. Eyeballing these measurements is not good enough.

2. Use the recommended thinner and equipment as specified by the manufacturer of the paint.

3. Air pressure is very important to a good paint job. Be sure you are using the proper recommended pressure at the gun by consulting the chart.

4. Experiment on an old piece of sheet metal to find the right combination of air pressure, distance and film thickness before you begin to paint.

5. Spray a light (fog) coat, followed by heavier, color coats.

6. Overlap the paint coats by 50% for best coverage.

7. Keep the gun moving at an even speed, perpendicular to the surface.

# ESTIMATED AIR PRESSURES AT THE GUN

Air pressure instructions are based on at-the-gun pressures. While the dial at the regulator indicates air pressure, there is a drop in air pressure at the gun, the amount of which is affected by the size and length of hose, snap hose connectors and hose conditions. For a close estimated at-the-gun pressure, this table may be used.

| Pressure Reading (Lbs.) At Gage | | Pressure At-The-Gun For Various Hose Lengths | | | | | |
|---|---|---|---|---|---|---|---|
| | | 5 ft | 10 ft | 15 ft | 20 ft | 25 ft | 50 ft |
| ¼ Inch Hose | 30 | 26 | 24 | 23 | 22 | 21 | 9 |
| | 40 | 34 | 32 | 31 | 29 | 27 | 16 |
| | 50 | 43 | 40 | 38 | 36 | 34 | 22 |
| | 60 | 51 | 48 | 46 | 43 | 41 | 29 |
| | 70 | 59 | 56 | 53 | 51 | 48 | 36 |
| | 80 | 68 | 64 | 61 | 58 | 55 | 43 |
| | 90 | 76 | 71 | 68 | 65 | 61 | 51 |
| ⁵⁄₁₆ Inch Hose | 30 | 29 | 28½ | 28 | 27½ | 27 | 23 |
| | 40 | 38 | 37 | 37 | 37 | 36 | 32 |
| | 50 | 48 | 47 | 46 | 46 | 45 | 40 |
| | 60 | 57 | 56 | 55 | 55 | 54 | 49 |
| | 70 | 66 | 65 | 64 | 63 | 63 | 57 |
| | 80 | 75 | 74 | 73 | 72 | 71 | 66 |
| | 90 | 84 | 83 | 82 | 81 | 80 | 74 |

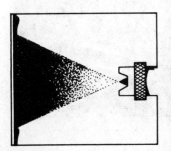 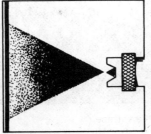 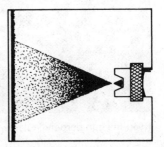

**WRONG**
Thin coat, rough, dry, no lustre.

**REASONS**
Gun too far away
Paint too thin
Too much air
Stroke too fast
Not enough overlap

**CORRECT**
Medium coat, good flow-out with hardly any orange peel and no sags.

**REASONS**
Gun clean and properly adjusted
Gun distance proper
Stroke okay
Overlap 50%

**WRONG**
Heavy coat with sags, ripples or orange peel.

**REASONS**
Dirty air nozzle
Gun too close
Paint too thin or too thick
Low air pressure
Stroke too slow
Too much overlap

Experiment on an old piece of sheet metal to get the right combination and "touch"

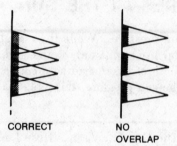

CORRECT          NO
                 OVERLAP

For good coverage, coats should be over-
lapped

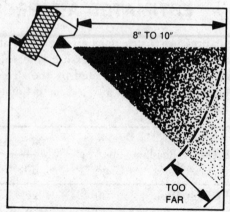

8" TO 10"

TOO
FAR

If the gun is not kept perpendicular to the surface, paint coverage will be spotty and thin in
places

Keep the gun perpendicular to the surface

# BLENDING THE NEW PAINT

For a practically invisible repair, it will be necessary to blend the new paint into the old using very fine rubbing compound.

The final paint coat should be allowed to dry for at least 48 hours (lacquer and acrylic) or 30 days (non-synthetic enamel) before using rubbing compound.

Wet the entire painted area thoroughly with water. Fold a clean cloth into a pad and work a *little* fine rubbing compound into the pad, which should be very wet. Don't use too much compound.

Lightly rub the entire panel, old and new finish, with horizontal strokes. Never use a circular motion. Start at the top of the panel and work to the bottom using lots of water. The panel will be left with a residue of compound which can be wiped off with a dry cloth, wiping in the same direction that you rubbed. Then wet a cloth and wipe the panel until all compound is gone.

Compare the smoothness of the surrounding paint and the new paint. It should be about even. If not, wet sand the new paint lightly with #600 paper, and compound again. Clean the area and buff it with a clean cloth until the entire panel has a uniform sheen.

Wash the panel clean and polish; unless you have used enamel paint, which should not be waxed for at least 6 months.

# SPECIAL PROBLEMS

## Clear Coat Paint

In recent years many car makers have been using a clear coat finish on many of their car lines. The end result is an eye catching depth to paint jobs, particularly to many of the metallic or irridescent glamor colors. But these clear coats are proving to be traps for the unwary repairing auto body damages. Here's why.

Many owners fail to realize that the vehicle had a clear coat on top of its color. This type of finish is known as 2-stage, or 2-phase.

Attempts to blend the new color through the original clear usually fail.

2-phase painting is not new. At the turn of the century painters were applying this system on cars, trucks, and carriages. Color was applied by brush. When it was fully dried, it was then sanded with pumice stone. Pumice cutting quality can be compared with a very fine sandpaper of approximately 1000 grit. When the painted surface was fully sanded and cleaned the paint would look extremely dull. Clear varnish was then brushed on. Instantly it brought out the color in full deep gloss. This system was, and still is, superior to the normal gloss that remains on just a color application. Wax and similar polishes applied on color can highlight the gloss, but they are not as lasting, or as glossy, as a clear finish can be.

Today, the 2-phase system is basically the same. Apply color, make sure its surface is free from all imperfections, and then apply a clear coat to magnify the color.

Clear varnish is no longer used for automotive applications. Today's clear is a see-through paint. There are various types of clears. There's a clear coat that is used as a protective coating on interior nonferrous metals like aluminum, a clear that covers and highlights a color, and a clear that can be used for blend coating.

Many cars arrive with OE (original equipment) clear coat finishes over the color coat. Just about the only way to know if a car you are working on has clear coat or not is to check in trunk and engine compartment areas for evidence of clear coat termination. You may be able to lift a small chip of clear off with a finger nail.

Look carefully for evidence of peeling at the edges of the original clear coat application on the car body. If a chip of clear coat can be pried away from the underlying color coat you've got a clear-coat-finished car on your hands.

For the inexperienced, it's possible to check if a car has a clear coat on it through the paint code, which will be found on the body number plate. Don't assume all late model cars—even metallic finishes—are clear coated. Check with the local car dealer of the brand in question or ask the body shop, if they have one, or the parts department, if the subject vehicle has OE clear coat on it.

This is a good example of a job that is not for the do-it-yourselfer. Application of clear coat paint and repainting of panels that are clear coated should be left to professionals.

## Stone Resistant Coatings

In recent model years cars have been arriving on the street with a new customer convenience option. It's a stone-chip resistant coating which preserves the cosmetic appearance of the lower body panels and protects them against stone damage—which can lead to rust damage. This new coating is virtually undetectable, and must be taken into account when making lower body damage repairs to a late-model car with this feature.

Some two years ago, car makers began applying a special coating between the metal and top coat. This abrasion-resistant coating may be called "stone-guard" or "gravel protector" finishes by some car makers. Whatever the name, the material used is usually a clear vinyl coating that is similar to smooth undercoating. The color coat is applied on top of the coating and thus becomes cushioned from stone pecking. If the paint does chip, the stone guard finish does not. Its basic purpose is to prevent rust from setting in.

This body repair person must be aware of this type of coating, because it is virtually impossible to feather-edge the lower areas. The sandpaper becomes quickly clogged, and blending just won't take. As with any other type of body and paint work, a lack of knowledge about any job can ensure its becoming a disaster. One method of testing is to press the surface with a pin. Remember the resistant coating is some 15 to 20 mils thick. It should have a cushiony feel.

Remove color and coating with a heat gun. Use a scraping tool to get the coating off once it is softened from the heat. *Be extremely careful that heat application does not cause metal warpage.*

After the bulk of the finish has been removed, clean the area with either a grinder or power sander.

This is an example of another paint job that should be left to a professional who has the skill and the experience to do a quality job.

# 17

# Body Care

Now that you've restored your car's body and paint to something resembling its original finish, you should give some thought to keeping it that way.

There are hundreds—maybe thousands—of products on the market, all designed to protect or aid your car's finish in some manner. There are as many different products as there are ways to use them, but they all have one thing in common— the surface must be clean.

## WASHING

The primary ingredient for washing your car is water, preferrably "soft" water. In many areas of the country, the local water supply is "hard" containing many minerals. The little rings or film that is left on your car's surface after it has dried is the result of "hard" water.

Since you usually can't change the local water supply, the next best thing is to dry the surface before it has a chance to dry itself.

Into the water you usually add soap. Don't use detergents or common, coarse soaps. Your car's paint never truly dries out, but is always evaporating residual oils into the air. Harsh detergents will remove these oils, causing the paint to dry faster than normal. Instead use warm water and a non-detergent soap made especially for waxed surfaces or a liquid soap made for waxed surfaces or a liquid soap made for washing dishes by hand. Other products that can be used on painted surfaces include baking soda or plain soda water for stubborn dirt.

Wash the car completely, starting at the top, and rinse it completely clean. Abrasive grit should be loaded off under water pressure; scrubbing them off will scratch the finish. The best washing tools are sponges, cleaning mitts or soft towels. Whatever you choose, replace it often as they tend to absorb grease and dirt.

Other ways to get a better wash include:

• Don't wash your car in the sun or when the finish is hot.

• Use water pressure to remove caked-on dirt.

•Remove tree-sap and bird effluence immediately. Such substances will eat through wax, polish and paint.

One of the best implements to dry your car is a turkish towel or an old, soft bath towel. Anything with a deep nap will hold any dirt in suspension and not grind it in to the paint.

Harder cloths will only grind the grit into the paint making more scratches. Always start drying at the top, followed by the hood and trunk and sides. You'll find there's always more dirt near the rocker panels and wheelwells which will wind up on the rest of the car if you dry these areas first.

# CLEANERS, WAXES AND POLISHES

Before going any farther you need to know the function of various products.

Cleaners—remove the top layer of dead pigment or paint.

Compounds—rubbing compounds are used to remove stubborn dirt, get rid of minor scratches, smooth away imperfections and partially restore badly weathered paint.

Polishes—polishes contain no abrasives or waxes; they shine the paint by adding oils to the paint.

Waxes—is a protective coating for the polish.

## Cleaners

Before you apply any wax, you'll have to remove oxidation, road film and other types of pollutants that simply washing will not remove.

The paint on your car never dries completely. There are always residual oils evaporating from the paint into the air. When enough oils are present in the paint, it has a healthy shine (gloss). When too many oils evaporate the paint takes on a whitish cast known as oxidation. The idea of polishing and waxing is to keep enough oil present in the painted surface to prevent oxidation, but when it occurs; the only recourse is to remove the top layer of "dead" paint, exposing the healthy paint underneath.

Products to remove oxidation and road film are sold under a variety of generic names—polishes, cleaner, rubbing compound, cleaner/polish, polish/cleaner, self-polishing wax, pre-wax cleaner, finish restorer and many more. Regardless of name there are two types of cleaners—abrasive cleaners (sometimes called polishing or rubbing compounds) that remove oxidation by grinding away the top layer of "dead" paint, or chemical cleaners that dissolve the "dead" pigment, allowing it to be wiped away.

Abrasive cleaners, by their nature, leave thousands of minute scratches in the finish, which must be polished out later. These should only be used in extreme cases, but are usually the only thing to use on badly oxidized paint finishes. Chemical cleaners are much milder but are not strong enough for severe cases of oxidation or weathered paint.

The most popular cleaners are liquid or paste abrasive polishing and rubbing compounds. Polishing compounds have a finer abrasive grit for medium duty work.

Rubbing compounds are a coarser abrasive and for heavy duty work. Unless you are familar with how to use compounds, be very careful. Excessive rubbing with any type of compound or cleaner can grind right through the paint to primer or bare metal. Follow the directions on the container—depending on type, the cleaner may or may not be OK for your paint. For example, some cleaners are not formulated for acrylic lacquer finishes.

When a small area needs compounding or heavy polishing, it's best to do the job by hand. Some people prefer a powered buffer for large areas. Avoid cutting through the paint along styling edges on the body. Small, hand operations where the compound is applied and rubbed using cloth folded into a thick ball, allow you to work in straight lines along such edges.

To avoid cutting through on the edges when using a power buffer, try masking tape. Just cover the edge with tape while using power. Then finish the job by hand with the tape removed. Even then work carefully. The paint tends to be a lot thinner along the sharp ridges stamped into the panels.

Compounding by machine or by hand, only work on a small area and apply the compound sparingly. If the materials are spread too thin, or allowed to sit too long, they dry out. Once dry they lose the ability to deliver a smooth, clean finish. Also, dried out polish tends to cause the buffer to stick in one spot. This in turn can burn or cut through the finish.

When rubbing out blemishes or just polishing paint, work in straight lines—there's less risk of rubbing through the paint

Use a polish or wax sparingly when power buffing. Liquid or paste should be spread evenly, because the pad must operate on wax or polish, not bare paint. If not, the pad could burn the paint

# BEFORE YOU BEGIN TO BUFF

Brighter shines and longer buffing bonnet life are well worth the extra effort it takes to keep the pads in good condition. Bonnets are usually either wool pile or lamb's wool. The pile bonnet will last longer than the lamb's wool, especially under constant use on a buffing machine. But the lamb's wool is softer and gives a glossier shine than pile. So lamb's wool is normally saved for the final finish of a wax job.

Poor care of a buffing bonnet not only shortens the life of the pad, but results in a poor polish job. Proper care, though, can nearly double the useful life of a bonnet.

Brand new bonnets especially those with finer texture, tend to lint. Before using one on a car, attach the bonnet to the machine and hold it against the edge of a work bench. Run the machine at about 500 rpm for a minute to remove most of the surface lint.

After buffing about four times remove the pad and clean it thoroughly. Use lukewarm water and a mild detergent. Never use hot water. It makes even pre-shrunk wool shrink more, and curls the edge as well.

A word of caution about synthetic buffing bonnets: they are not intended for direct use on a car's finish. They are quite abrasive and can cut away the topmost layer of paint.

## Waxes and Polishes

Your car's finish can be protected in a number of ways. A cleaner/wax or polish/cleaner followed by wax or variations of each all provide good results. The 2-step approach (polish followed by wax) is probably slightly better but consumes more time and effort. Properly fed with oils, your paint should never need cleaning, but despite the best polishing job, it won't last unless it's protected with wax. Without wax polish must be renewed at least once a month to prevent oxidation. Years ago (some still swear by it today), the best wax was made from the Brazilian

### WAX, WHAT IT IS

Hydrocarbon is found in a lot of places but the most interesting variety for people trying to preserve paint is a Brazilian palm called the Carnauba. The vegetable wax extracted from this plant has an unusually high melting point, 185°F.

The thing that makes wax so good for protecting surfaces is its hydrophobic character—it rejects water. And the things which cause paint to deteriorate include water, light and air.

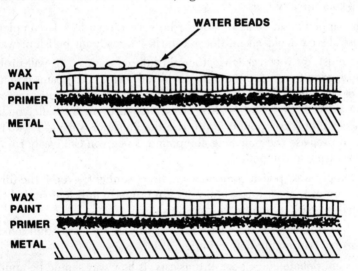

The film of wax applied to a surface will not exclude these completely, but it does slow the attack. Detergents tend to remove wax in spite of the fact that it will not readily dissolve in water. To help it get through several washings, a chemical called aminofunctional-silicones is added to the blend of waxes. The wax is blended to get toughness in an extremely thin film.

The layer of wax is perhaps only one molecule thick at some points. While this is difficult to measure, it isn't hard to detect. And the method used even by experts is the water beading test. If water "beads" on the surface, the wax layer is present. If it doesn't bead, it's time to clean and wax again.

palm, the Carnuba, favored for its vegetable base and high melting point. However, modern synthetic waxes are harder, which means they protect against moisture better, and chemically inert silicone is used for a long lasting protection. The only problem with silicone wax is that it penetrates all layers of paint. To repaint or touch up a panel or car protected by silicone wax, you have to completely strip the finish to avoid "fisheyes."

Under normal conditions, silicone waxes will last 4–6 months, but you have to be careful of wax build-up from too much waxing. Too thick a coat of wax is just as bad as no wax at all; it stops the paint from breathing.

Combination cleaners/waxes have become popular lately because they remove the old layer of wax plus light oxidation, while putting on a fresh coat of wax at the same time. Some cleaners/waxes contain abrasive cleaners which require caution, although many cleaner/waxes use a chemical cleaner.

## APPLYING WAX OR POLISH

You may view polishing and waxing your car as a pleasant way to spend an afternoon, or as a boring chore, but it has to be done to keep the paint on your car. Caring for the paint doesn't require special tools, but you should follow a few rules.

1. Use a good quality wax.

2. Before applying any wax or polish, be sure the surface is completely clean. Just because the car looks clean, doesn't mean it's ready for polish or wax.

3. If the finish on your car is weathered, dull, or oxidized, it will probably have to be compounded to remove the old or oxidized paint. If the paint is simply dulled from lack of care, one of the non-abrasive cleaners known as polishing compounds will do the trick. If the paint is severely scratched or really dull, you'll probably have to use a rubbing compound to prepare the finish for waxing. If you're not sure which one to use, use the polishing compound, since you can easily ruin the finish by using too strong a compound.

4. Don't apply wax, polish compound in direct sunlight, even if the directions on the can say you can. Most waxes will not cure properly in bright sunlight and you'll probably end up with a blotchy looking finish.

5. Don't rub the wax off too soon. The result will be a wet, dull looking finish. Let the wax dry thoroughly before buffing it off.

6. A constant debate among car enthusiasts, is how wax should be applied. Some maintain pastes or liquids should be applied in a circular motion, but body shop experts have long thought that this approach results in barely detectable circular abrasions, especially on cars that are waxed frequently. They advise rubbing in straight lines, especially if any kind of cleaner is involved.

7. If an applicator is not supplied with the wax, use a piece of soft cheesecloth or very soft lint-free material. The same applies to buffing the surface.

### Special Surfaces

One-step combination cleaner and wax formulas shouldn't be used on many of the special surfaces which abound on cars. The one-step materials contain abrasives to achieve a clean surface under the wax top coat. The abrasives are so mild that you could clean a car every week for a couple of years without fear of rubbing through the paint. But this same level of abrasiveness might, through repeated use, damage decals used for special trim effects. This includes wide stripes, wood-grain trim and other appliques.

Painted plastics must be cleaned with care. If a cleaner is too aggressive it will cut through the paint and expose the primer. If bright trim such as polish aluminum or chrome is painted, cleaning must be performed with even greater care. If rubbing compound is being used, it will cut faster than polish. Thus the possibility of getting into trouble is increased.

If you attempt to protect these more-porous-than-usual surfaces don't turn to low-luster furniture waxes. They aren't formulated for automotive finishes. They may even cause damage.

Just the opposite gloss problem is found with acrylic finishes. They have their highest gloss as sprayed. Abrasive cleaners will dull the finish. The best way to clean these newer finishes is with a non-abrasive liquid polish. Only dirt and oxidation, not paint, will be removed.

Taking a few minutes to read the instructions on the can of polish or wax will help prevent making serious mistakes. The information on the label is there because it is important. Not all preparations will work on all surfaces. And some are intended for power application while others will only work when applied by hand.

Don't get the idea that just pouring on some polish and then hitting it with a buffer will suffice. Power equipment speeds the operation. But it also adds a measure of risk. It's very easy to damage the finish if you use the wrong methods or materials.

### Caring for Chrome

The same advice applies to normal cleaning of chrome as well as paint, but there are special products for chrome if you live in areas where rust forms easily (shore, heavy rain or snow areas).

Read the label on the container. Many products are formulated specifically for chrome, but others contain abrasives that will scratch the chrome finish. If it isn't recommended for chrome, don't use it.

Never use steel wool or kitchen soap pads to clean chrome. Be careful not to get chrome cleaner on paint or interior vinyl surfaces. If you do, get it off immediately.

# INTERIOR CARE

One way to preserve the new car feeling is to keep the interior clean and protected. You have to use some common sense and not let the dirt accumulate. The more dirt that gets ground into carpeting and seats, the faster they will wear out. Keep the seats wiped down and the rugs vacuumed.

## Cleaning Fabric and Vinyl

There are a number of products on the market that will clean vinyl or fabric interiors, but mild soap and water is still one of the best (and cheapest) cleaners and should be used at least 3–4 times a year. Household cleaners like 409, Fantastik and multi-purpose cleaners such as Armor All® will also clean vinyl well. As with any cleaner, test it in an out-of-the-way place, before using it.

A whisk broom or vacuum cleaner will keep the rugs clean and free of loose dirt build-up. To clean the carpet, rug shampoo can be used as well as the foamy types in an aerosol can, but the foam types are more of a spot cleaner than an overall cleaner. When working with chemicals and spot removers, be sure that you follow directions on the product and work in a well ventilated area.

## HOW TO REMOVE STAINS FROM FABRIC INTERIOR

For best results, spots and stains should be removed as soon as possible. Never use gasoline, lacquer thinner, acetone, nail polish remover or bleach. Use a 3″ x 3″ piece of cheesecloth. Squeeze most of the liquid from the fabric and wipe the stained fabric from the outside of the stain toward the center with a lifting motion. Turn the cheesecloth as soon as one side becomes soiled. When using water to remove a stain, be sure to wash the entire section after the spot has been removed to avoid water stains. Encrusted spots can be broken up with a dull knife and vacuumed before removing the stain.

| Type of Stain | How to Remove It |
| --- | --- |
| Surface spots | Brush the spots out with a small hand brush or use a commercial preparation such as K2R to lift the stain. |
| Mildew | Clean around the mildew with warm suds. Rinse in cold water and soak the mildew area in a solution of 1 part table salt and 2 parts water. Wash with upholstery cleaner. |
| Water stains | Water stains in fabric materials can be removed with a solution made from 1 cup of table salt dissolved in 1 quart of water. Vigorously scrub the solution into the stain and rinse with clear water. Water stains in nylon or other synthetic fabrics should be removed with a commercial type spot remover. |
| Chewing gum, tar, crayons, shoe polish (greasy stains) | Do not use a cleaner that will soften gum or tar. Harden the deposit with an ice cube and scrape away as much as possible with a dull knife. Moisten the remainder with cleaning fluid and scrub clean. |
| Ice cream, candy | Most candy has a sugar base and can be removed with a cloth wrung out in warm water. Oily candy, after cleaning with warm water, should be cleaned with upholstery cleaner. Rinse with warm water and clean the remainder with cleaning fluid. |

| Type of Stain | How to Remove It |
|---|---|
| Wine, alcohol, egg, milk, soft drink (non-greasy stains) | Do not use soap. Scrub the stain with a cloth wrung out in warm water. Remove the remainder with cleaning fluid. |
| Grease, oil, lipstick, butter and related stains | Use a spot remover to avoid leaving a ring. Work from the outside of the stain to the center and dry with a clean cloth when the spot is gone. |
| Headliners (cloth) | Mix a solution of warm water and foam upholstery cleaner to give thick suds. Use only foam—liquid may streak or spot. Clean the entire headliner in one operation using a circular motion with a natural sponge. |
| Headliner (vinyl) | Use a vinyl cleaner with a sponge and wipe clean with a dry cloth. |
| Seats and door panels | Mix 1 pint upholstery cleaner in 1 gallon of water. Do not soak the fabric around the buttons. |
| Leather or vinyl fabric | Use a multi-purpose cleaner full strength and a stiff brush. Let stand 2 minutes and scrub thoroughly. Wipe with a clean, soft rag. |
| Nylon or synthetic fabrics | For normal stains, use the same procedures you would for washing cloth upholstery. If the fabric is extremely dirty, use a multi-purpose cleaner full strength with a stiff scrub brush. Scrub thoroughly in all directions and wipe with a cotton towel or soft rag. |

## Repairing Seats and Dash

Vinyl seats and dash are subject to cracking and tearing with hard use. Wear and tear in those areas is very noticeable but not too difficult to repair. Cloth covered seats are harder to repair, unless you're handy with a tailor's needle and thread. If you're not and the seams are coming apart, invest in a set of seat covers in lieu of a trip the the upholstery shop.

Any retail auto store sells pre-fitted seat covers at a fraction of the cost of new upholstery. Seat covers are sold as "fits-all" (universal application) or more expensively by make and model of car. Be sure to check if the covers fit bench or bucket seats, or split back seats. The covers are tied or wired under the seats.

Burn marks in vinyl seats, arm-rests and dashboards can be repaired with the help of a good vinyl repair kit. Rips in the vinyl and seams that have come apart are slightly more difficult but are well worth the time and effort in the end.

About the best way to repair a rip is to heat both sides of the tear with a hair drier. Lift up the material and place a 2″ wide strip of fabric tape under one side of the vinyl.

Stretch the other side over the tape and line it up carefully. When you have it lined up, press down. Hold it in place while someone applies the vinyl repair liquid over the area to be repaired. Let it dry completely before using it. The repair should look like new and last quite a while.

Other methods of repairing vinyl involve vinyl repair compounds that require heat. The kits contain a repair compound, applicator and several different graining papers. If the hole is deep, it will have to be filled with foam or anything to provide a backing.

## Rug Care

Before doing anything about cleaning carpets, thoroughly vacuum everything to remove all loose dirt. The foaming type of rug shampoo (aerosol cans) are good for spot cleaning.

Overall cleaning can be done with 1 pint of upholstery cleaner in 1 gallon of water. If the carpet is faded, spotted, or discolored, add an upholstery tint to the solution. To get the right color shade add tint in small quantities and test the solution by dipping a white cloth in and wringing it out. The color will usually dry a shade or 2 darker.

Apply the solution with a stiff brush and scrub the carpet vigorously, in one direction. When it dries, fluff the carpet with a dry brush.

Salt stains (from winter weather) can be removed by soaking the stained area in a heavy solution of table salt and water. Soak the stained area to loosen embedded salt with a stiff brush, if necessary, and wash the entire carpet. You may have to repeat this several times.

## Glass

Interior glass should be cleaned at least once a week to remove deposits from smoke and other films.

Water alone will seldom cut through the haze from cigarette smoke and usually only succeeds in rearranging the film.

Household, blue-liquid cleaners for glass work best. In the absence of these, or for stubborn dirt, use about 4 tablespoons of ammonia in 1 quart of water.

Clean the excess dirt and grime with a paper towel. Apply the cleaner and use a paper towel to clean the dust and dirt from the glass and another to polish the glass.

To remove overspray and masking tape residue from glass, use a strong professional type glass cleaner.

Exterior glass surfaces are best cleaned with commercial window cleaning solutions. Smears, bugs and road tar can be removed with a rubber or plastic scraper and window cleaner. Don't use razor blades (except as below), putty knives or steel wool.

To remove stubborn stickers, scotch tape or masking tape, wet a paper towel or cloth with cigarette lighter fluid and moisten the residue.

Let it soak in and very carefully scrape it away with a single edge razor blade. Stubborn stickers can also be removed by heating them with a hair drier to soften the adhesive.

## Clear Plastic

If you have any clear plastic, use a plastic cleaner that has no harsh abrasives. Inexpensive plastic polishes are available that will remove minor scratches and restore the finish.

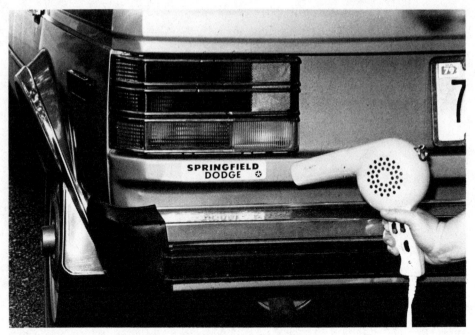

A hair drier will often soften the adhesive used to apply stickers

## Keeping the Interior Clean

Once you've gone to the trouble of cleaning up the interior, it'll be worth your while to keep it clean. It makes it much easier to clean up the next time around.

Common sense plus these tips will help keep the interior clean.

•Vacuum the carpets regularly. The hardest thing to get out of carpets is ground in dirt.

•If you don't have floor mats, invest in a set. They are a lot cheaper to replace than carpets and take a lot of wear the carpets would normally get.

•Don't be too heavy handed with waxes, polishes and dressings. Too much build-up of wax and polish only traps more dirt.

•Don't use dressings or wax on dirty vinyl. Spend a little time to clean it properly before applying a vinyl dressing.

•A combination cleaner/protectant or saddle soap used on vinyl will keep it soft and pliable, but will also make the seats slippery. A good buffing with a soft cloth will reduce the slippery feeling.

•If your fabric upholstery is fairly new, and absolutely clean, Scotchguarding® will keep stains from setting in the fabric and make them easier to clean. But, if the fabric is already dirty or old, you're only wasting your time.

•If possible, park your car in the shade. If you can't park in the shade, at least cover the seat back and dash if they will be in the sun's rays.

•Clean spots and stains as quickly as possible before they have a chance to set in the material. You stand a better chance of completely removing the stain if you remove it while it's wet.

# Auto Body Refinishing Terms

**Abrasive**—A hard grit used for sanding or grinding

**Adhesion**—The ability of the paint or primer to stick to the surface to which it is applied

**Air-dry**—Allowing paint to dry at ambient (surrounding) temperatures, without the aid of an external heat source

**Aluminum oxide**—A metallic abrasive used to manufacture sandpaper and sanding discs

**Atomize**—The extent to which a spray gun breaks up paint into a fine mist, fog or spray

**Binder**—The ingredient in a paint that holds the pigment particles together

**Bleeding**—A lower (older) color coming through a fresh coat of paint

**Blistering**—The formation of bubbles on the paint surface

**Blushing**—The formation of a whitish or misty appearance on the finish color

**Chalking**—The appearance of a white powder of a paint surface as it weathers and ages

**Checking**—Short, very fine crack lines that appear in the paint film

**Compound**—An abrasive paste or liquid that smooths and polishes the painted surface

**Crazing**—Many fine cracks in the paint surface, resembling crow's feet

**Cross-hatch coat**—Checkerboard application of paint to be sure of a continuous paint film. One medium coat is usually followed by a second medium coat in a perpendicular direction

**Curing**—The final drying stage where the paint reaches maximum strength

**De-grease**—Wiping with a clean cloth saturated in a solvent. This is essential to good paint adhesion

**Die-back**—In a lacquer finish, the loss of gloss after compounding, caused by continued evaporation of thinner

**Dry-spray**—Atomized paint that does nt dissolve into the material being sprayed. It is caused by holding the gun too far from the work, too much air pressure or a solvent that evaporates too fast

**Evaporation**—Solvents in the paint escaping to the air

**Feather-edge**—The tapered edge of the paint where it meets the metal. The edges should be tapered or slanted so that no edge will be felt when a finger is passed over it

**Ferrous metals**—Metals made from iron (steel). Non-ferrous metals are aluminum alloys, brass, copper or magnesium

**Finish coat**—The final color coat

**Fish eyes**—Small pits that form in the finish coat, usually due to insufficient or improper cleaning of the old coat

**Flash**—The fits stage of the drying process where most of the solvent evaporates

**Flash time**—The time required for a coat of paint to lose most of its solvent through evaporation

**Fog coat**—A fully reduced (thinned) paint that is sprayed at higher than normal air pressure or with the gun held at a greater distance than normal from the work. The object is to obtain a fast flash-off (evaporation) of thinner with minimum penetration of thinner into the old paint

**Glazing**—Use of special putty to fill minor imperfections

**Gloss**—The ability of a paint to reflect images when polished

**Hardener**—Chemical added to plastic filler to induce hardening

**Hiding**—The ability of a paint to obscure the surface to which it is applied

**Metallic paint**—Finish paint colors that contain metallic flakes in addition to pigment

**Mist coat**—Usually the final color coat, produced by over-reducing with a slow evaporating thinner. It is generally used to blend in the final overlap areas

**OEM**—Original Equipment Manufacturer

**Orange peel**—A rough paint surface, resembling the skin of an orange caused by the paint spray failing to flow together

**Original finish**—The paint applied to vehicle when it is built by the manufacturer

**Overlap**—The part of the spray band that covers the previous application of paint. A 50% overlap on each stroke is generally recommended

**Overspray**—The fine mist of paint on areas where it is not wanted (glass, moldings, other painted surfaces, etc). The tell-tale mark of a car that has been painted or had body work done

**Oxidation**—One of the processes by which enamel paint cures, by combining oxygen in the air with the paint film. This process dries and continues to harden enamel for several weeks. Oxidation also results in chalking in older paint

**Paint film**—The actual thickness of the paint on a surface

**Pigment**—Finely ground powders in the paint that give it its color

**Prime coat**—Primer or surfacer applied to the old paint or bare metal before the finish coat is applied

**Primer**—The surfacer that acts as a bond between the metal surface or old paint and the color coat

**Reducer**—The solvent that is used to thin enamel

**Sanding block**—A block of rubber or plastic to which the sandpaper is fastened, offering the operator a good grip. The block should be used for most sanding jobs because it distributes the pressure evenly and gives a more uniform surface

**Sand scratches**—The marks left in metal or in the old finish by abrasives. They may also show in the finish coat due to lack of filling or sealing

**Sand scratch swelling**—Solvents present in surface scratches that cause the old finish to swell

**Sealer**—An intercoat between the top coat and the primer or old finish, giving better adhesion

**Settling**—Pigment in the paint collecting at the bottom of the spray gun container

**Shrinkage**—The shrinking of automotive paint as it dries. All automotive paints shrink, and if scratches or surface imperfections have not been properly filled, they will show up as the paint shrinks into them

**Single coat**—A coat of paint, with each stroke overlapping the previous stroke by 50%

**Solids**—The ingredients (pigments and binders) of the paint that remain on the surface after the solvents evaporate

**Solvents**—A fluid that dilutes, liquefies or dilutes another liquid or solid. Solvents include thinners, reducers and cleaners

**Spot glazing**—Filling minor imperfections (sand scratches)

**Substrate**—The surface that is to be finished (painted). It can be anything from an old finish or primer to an unpainted surface

**Surface dry**—A condition in which the outer layer (surface) of the finish dries while the underneath remain soft and not thoroughly dried

**Stress lines**—Low areas in a damaged panel, usually starting at the point of impact and travelling outward

**Tack coat**—The first coat of enamel that is allowed to dry until "tacky" usually about 10–30 minutes, depending on the amount of thinner used. The surface is "tacky" when it will not stick to the finger when light pressure is applied

**Tack rag**—A cloth impregnated with a non-drying varnish that is used to pick up dust and dirt particles

**Thinner**—The solvent used to thin lacquers and enamels to the proper consistency for application

**Undercoats**—All of the products used to prepare the surface to receive color coats (primers, surfacers, putties, sealers, etc.)

**Water-spotting**—Drops of water that mar the finish before it is thoroughly cured

**Weathering**—The change in appearance of paint caused by exposure to the elements

# Chilton's Repair & Tune-Up Guides

## The complete line covers domestic cars, imports, trucks, vans, RV's and 4-wheel drive vehicles.

| CODE | TITLE |
|------|-------|
| #7199 | AMC 75–82; all models |
| #7165 | Alliance 1983 |
| #7323 | Aries 81–82 |
| #7344 | Arrow 78–83 |
| #7193 | Aspen/Volaré 76–80 |
| #5902 | Audi 70–73 |
| #7028 | Audi 4000/5000 77–81 |
| #6337 | Audi Fox 73–75 |
| #5807 | Barracuda 65–72 |
| #7203 | Blazer 69–82 |
| #5576 | BMW 59–70 |
| #7315 | BMW 70–82 |
| #7308 | Buick 75–83 all full sized models |
| #7307 | Buick Century/Regal 75–83 |
| #7045 | Camaro 67–81 |
| #7317 | Camaro 82–83 |
| #6695 | Capri 70–77 |
| #7195 | Capri 79–82 |
| #7059 | Cavalier 1982 |
| #7309 | Celebrity 82–83 |
| #7309 | Century 82–83 |
| #5807 | Challenger 65–72 |
| #7343 | Challenger (Import) 71–83 |
| #7344 | Champ 78–83 |
| #6316 | Charger/Coronet 71–75 |
| #7162 | Chevette 76–82 inc. diesel |
| #7313 | Chevrolet 68–83 all full sized models |
| #7167 | Chevrolet/GMC Pick-Ups 70–82 |
| #7169 | Chevrolet/GMC Vans 67–82 |
| #7310 | Chevrolet S-10/GMC S-15 Pick-Ups 82–83 |
| #7051 | Chevy Luv 72–81 inc. 4wd |
| #7056 | Chevy Mid-Size 64–81 inc. El Camino, Chevelle, Laguna, Malibu & Monte Carlo |
| #6841 | Chevy II 62–79 |
| #7309 | Ciera 82–83 |
| #7059 | Cimarron 1982 |
| #7335 | Citation 80–83 |
| #7343 | Colt 71–83 |
| #7194 | Continental 1982 |
| #6691 | Corvair 60–69 inc. Turbo |
| #6576 | Corvette 53–62 |
| #7192 | Corvette 63–82 |
| #7405 | Cougar 65–73 |
| #7190 | Cutlass 70–82 |
| #6324 | Dart/Demon 68–76 |
| #5790 | Datsun 61–72 |
| #7196 | Datsun F10, 310, Nissan Stanza 77–82 |
| #7170 | Datsun 200SX, 510, 610, 710, 810 73–82 |
| #7197 | Datsun 1200, 210/Nissan Sentra 73–82 |
| #7172 | Datsun Z & ZX 70–82 |
| #7050 | Datsun Pick-Ups 70–81 inc. 4wd |
| #6554 | Dodge 68–77 all full sized models |
| #7323 | Dodge 400 1982 |
| #6486 | Dodge Charger 67–70 |
| #7168 | Dodge Vans 67–82 |
| #7032 | Dodge D-50/Plymouth Arrow Pick-Ups 77–81 |
| #7055 | Escort 81–82 inc. EXP & LN-7 |
| #6320 | Fairlane/Torino 62–75 |
| #7312 | Fairmont 78–83 |
| #7042 | Fiat 69–81 |
| #6846 | Fiesta 78–80 |
| #7046 | Firebird 67–81 |
| #7345 | Firebird 82–83 |
| #7059 | Firenza 1982 |
| #7318 | Ford 68–83 all full sized models |
| #7140 | Ford Bronco 66–81 |
| #7341 | Ford Courier 72–82 |
| #7194 | Ford Mid-Size 71–82 inc. Torino, Gran Torino, Ranchero, Elite, LTD II & Thunderbird |
| #7166 | Ford Pick-Ups 65–82 inc. 4wd |
| #7171 | Ford Vans 61–82 |
| #7165 | Fuego 82–83 |
| #6935 | GM Sub-compact 71–81 inc. Vega, Monza, Astre, Sunbird, Starfire & Skyhawk |
| #7311 | Granada 78–83 |
| #7204 | Honda 73–82 |
| #5912 | International Scout 67–73 |
| #7136 | Jeep CJ 1945–81 |
| #6739 | Jeep Wagoneer, Commando, Cherokee 66–79 |
| #7203 | Jimmy 69–82 |
| #7059 | J-2000 1982 |
| #7165 | Le Car 76–83 |
| #7323 | Le Baron 1982 |
| #7055 | Lynx 81–82 inc. EXP & LN-7 |
| #6634 | Maverick/Comet 70–77 |
| #7198 | Mazda 71–82 |
| #7031 | Mazda RX-7 79–81 |
| #6065 | Mercedes-Benz 59–70 |
| #5907 | Mercedes-Benz 68–73 |
| #6809 | Mercedes-Benz 74–79 |
| #7318 | Mercury 68–83 all full sized models |
| #7194 | Mercury Mid-Size 71–82 inc. Continental, Cougar, XR-7 & Montego |
| #7173 | MG 61–80 |
| #7311 | Monarch 75–80 |
| #7405 | Mustang 65–73 |
| #6812 | Mustang II 74–78 |
| #7195 | Mustang 79–82 |
| #6841 | Nova 69–79 |
| #7308 | Oldsmobile 75–83 all full sized models |
| #7335 | Omega 80–83 |
| #7191 | Omni/Horizon 78–82 |
| #6575 | Opel 71–75 |
| #5982 | Peugeot 70–74 |
| #7335 | Phoenix 80–83 |
| #7027 | Pinto/Bobcat 71–80 |
| #8552 | Plymouth 68–76 full sized models |
| #7168 | Plymouth Vans 67–82 |
| #7308 | Pontiac 75–83 all full sized models |
| #7309 | Pontiac 6000 82–83 |
| #5822 | Porsche 69–73 |
| #7048 | Porsche 924 & 928 77–81 inc. Turbo |
| #7323 | Reliant 81–82 |
| #7165 | Renault 75–83 |
| #7383 | S-10 Blazer 82–83 |
| #7383 | S-15 Jimmy 82–83 |
| #5988 | Saab 69–75 |
| #7344 | Sapporo 78–83 |
| #5821 | Satellite/Roadrunner, Belvedere, GTX 68–73 |
| #7059 | Skyhawk 1982 |
| #7335 | Skylark 80–83 |
| #7208 | Subaru 70–82 |
| #5905 | Tempest/GTO/LeMans 68–73 |
| #5795 | Toyota 66–70 |
| #7314 | Toyota Celica & Supra 71–83 |
| #7316 | Toyota Corolla, Carina, Tercel, Starlet 70–83 |
| #7044 | Toyota Corona, Cressida, Crown, Mark II 70–81 |
| #7035 | Toyota Pick-Ups 70–81 |
| #5910 | Triumph 69–73 |
| #7162 | T-1000 1982 |
| #6326 | Valiant/Duster 68–76 |
| #5796 | Volkswagen 49–71 |
| #6837 | Volkswagen 70–81 |
| #7339 | Volkswagen Front Wheel Drive 74–83 inc. Dasher, GTI, Jetta, Quantum, Pick-Up, Rabbit, Scirocco |
| #6529 | Volvo 56–69 |
| #7040 | Volvo 70–80 |
| #7312 | Zephyr 78–83 |

Chilton's Repair & Tune-Up Guides are available at your local retailer or by mailing a check or money order for **$11.95** plus **$1.00** to cover postage and handling to:

## Chilton Book Company
### Dept. DM
### Radnor, PA 19089

**NOTE:** When ordering be sure to include your name & address, book code & title.